Surreal Change

In *Surreal Change: The Real Life of Transforming Public Education*, internationally renowned expert Michael Fullan reflects on the leading trends and ideas within the educational change field over a 50-year period. The author traces the evolution of the field through his own personal developments and contributions to it, working chronologically through "The 12 Seminal Ideas" of his career. Fullan shows his personal and vulnerable side as well as how he came to develop breakthrough ideas. By looking at the way the field has transformed and grown over time, Fullan draws attention to what ideas have persisted, what problems still need solving, and what faces teachers, leaders and reformers today. Deeply personal and insightful, *Surreal Change* contextualizes the past, present, and future of school reform to help leaders continue to bring about lasting, positive, systemic change in their organization.

Michael Fullan, Order of Canada, is Professor Emeritus at the University of Toronto and the former Dean of the Ontario Institute for Studies in Education of the University of Toronto. He is policy advisor to the Premier and the Minister of Education, Ontario. He is known internationally as an innovative leader in leadership and system change. He participates as a researcher, consultant, trainer, and policy advisor on many educational change initiatives with school systems, teachers' federations, research institutes, and government agencies. His latest book (with Quinn and McEachen) is *Deep Learning: Engage the World Change the World*.

Routledge Leading Change Series
Edited by Andy Hargreaves and Pak Tee Ng

Surreal Change

The Real Life of Transforming Public Education

Michael Fullan

Routledge
Taylor & Francis Group

NEW YORK AND LONDON

First published 2018
by Routledge
711 Third Avenue, New York, NY 10017

and by Routledge
2 Park Square, Milton Park, Abingdon, Oxon, OX14 4RN

Routledge is an imprint of the Taylor & Francis Group, an informa business

Library of Congress Cataloging-in-Publication Data
Names: Fullan, Michael, author.
Title: Surreal change: the real life of transforming public
education / Michael Fullan.
Description: New York, NY: Routledge, 2018. |
Includes bibliographical references and index.
Identifiers: LCCN 2017052863 | ISBN 9781138926837
(hbk: alk. paper) | ISBN 9781138926844 (pbk: alk. paper) |
ISBN 9781315682952 (ebk)
Subjects: LCSH: Education and state–Canada–History. |
Public schools–Canada–History. | Educational
sociology–Canada–History. | Fullan, Michael. |
Educators–Canada–Biography. | Sociologists–Canada–Biography.
Classification: LCC LC91.F85 2018 | DDC 379.20971–dc23
LC record available at https://lccn.loc.gov/2017052863

ISBN: 978-1-138-92683-7 (hbk)
ISBN: 978-1-138-92684-4 (pbk)
ISBN: 978-1-315-68295-2 (ebk)

Typeset in Caslon
by Sunrise Setting Ltd., Brixham, UK

To Vince, Mary, Gerry, and Harry
Together at last!

Contents

1

SURREAL CHANGE

Surreal change: Having the disorienting, hallucinating quality of a dream; unreal, fantastic

In 2014 Andy Hargreaves invited me to write a book for his Routledge *Leading Change Series* that would focus on the change ideas that I had lived through, and in some cases developed, over the decades of my career. The idea was to link the person to the ideas, and vice versa. This then is a very different book—an experiment in writing. I was never reluctant to take this on but somehow I was not getting around to starting the book. Maybe I wanted it to be a round 50 years of professional work— 1968–2018. Or perhaps I was procrastinating not wanting to intimate that I was nearing the end. My best form of procrastination was to write another book. Finally in August 2017 I decided that I had better do it or it would never happen. Immediately I had two great ideas for two new books. One, I called *Nuance*—what is it that especially effective leaders know and do that other leaders can't seem to emulate. The other is about large-scale change that I wanted to do with my close colleague, Mary Jean Gallagher and titled *System change: The devil is in the details.*

But this time I got wise. I did some integrative thinking and concluded that there is no reason that I could not work on my autobiography and the two new books simultaneously. In fact it seemed appropriate to the weird 'surreal' life I had been living for my professional career, namely that I would finish by never finishing, and that

I would have several irons in the fire. So, my plan is to write three books in parallel. I have not yet written the first word of either of the other two books, and you won't hear about them again until the postscript. I will let you know how they turned out.

This is a 'professional' autobiography, which means that I will be focusing on my life only insofar as it relates to the ideas and actions that I have been pursuing over 50 years. In this respect it will be personal, and I will strive to be transparent and vulnerable when the circumstances call for it (recognizing that most of us are inevitably self-serving when it comes to explaining our actions). I won't refer to professional awards, recognitions, honorary doctorates and the like unless they are directly related to the specific change ideas associated with my ideas and development.

As for my personal life, I am 77 years old as I write this, have been married twice with a total of five children who range from 26 to 50 years of age, and generally would be considered a workaholic. I met my first wife, Sylvia, at the University of Toronto, and we married in 1966. We have three children: Chris, Maureen, and Josh. We have three grand-children: Daniel (18) and Peter (15), sons of Maureen and her husband, Wayne Egan; and a girl, Maddie, born to Josh and Jae on September 4, 2017 just as I was finishing this book. My second marriage was to Wendy in 1980 and we have two children: Bailey (34) and Conor (26). You will find more of the personal me in the subsequent chapters, although more about the professional side than the family activities. You should find out enough to figure out my personality. For starters, for example, is my workaholicism, which might be about committing to 'things', rather than to people that would require personal commitment.

This brief introduction is philosophical, and intended to provide a permeable, atmospheric, quality to my development. It seemed like the things that happened to me in my life were not a result of any planning (at least not on my part). Things happened and *then* I would make sense of them. In many ways the notion that 'things happen' is an apt metaphor for the concept of change itself. The moment you over plan change is when it starts to go off the rails. If you want to kill a good idea mandate it.

Luck played a huge role in my life. Things happened that should not have ended well, but at the last moment they did. It took more than 25 years to have even a glimpse of what I might want to do. Increasingly the concept of change chased me not vice versa. Expressing or even having *feelings* has been missing most of my life. Yet, I found myself increasingly attuned to what I would call 'cognitive empathy'. I could understand where most people were coming from. Making a positive difference in other people's lives has become a large part of my life's work, but if truth were to be told I became deeply committed to things not just because I want to do good, but because it turns me on to solve complex problems. Eventually moral purpose and trying to solve complex human problems on a large scale merged into my life. But this was not the driver early on. At the early stage there was no driver. It was 'me being me'—drifting, and latching on to things out of survival or budding interest.

Another serendipitous thing is being born in exactly the right time and right place. Coming into this world in 1940 was not great if you were living in Europe but in Toronto, Canada being fortunate was being raised for the first five years by a group of caring women—my mother, great aunts, and great grandmother. My great aunts were Anna and Gertrude, and my great grandmother was Elizabeth (called Margaret) Fitzpatrick. All of them including my mother were my first mentors. Imagine being alive in 2018 (me), and being able to say that I was mentored by my great grandmother who was born in 1858! She died when I was 13 years old so I did experience a strong piece of what I remember as my 'always old' aunts and great grandmother.

Growing up in the 1950s seemed idyllic. After a few self-imposed bumps as we will see in Chapter 1, I drifted into a Ph.D as a default option, landed a university job as a junior professor without ever applying for it, and started a career at exactly the time to witness the birth of the concept of *implementation*. None of this was conscious. It only makes sense in retrospect. And today when a colleague ends up in remote northern Pakistan near the Chinese border that you can only reach by helicopter, and sees a sign at the entrance of the village where written in chalk is a change saying attributed to Michael Fullan, and you realize that it is something you never said or wrote—the word surreal comes to mind.

What was this 50-year journey, what were the key ideas, and how do they interface with what is happening and evolving in the world? This book is about change ideas in different decades of time—ideas that took their shape because of the particular moment in history in which they occurred, and that shaped but did not determine subsequent developments. I will try to identify milestone ideas that seemed then, or now, prominent to me. I was there! I will mark and number these ideas as they occur chronologically as *Seminal Idea #1* and so on. There will be 12 of them in total. Not that they were brilliant ideas in each case, but they were key to my development and eventually as a set they became seminal for me and to a certain extent the field.

Increasingly, in leadership positions I came to realize what Kurt Lewin meant when he said that "if you truly want to understand something try changing it". My colleagues and I did and are trying to change a lot, and we are indeed learning an enormous amount. But it is often a blur when it is occurring. Insights come but they are based on imagined patterns as much as on reality. When one realizes that there is often little difference between real time and surreal time, you know that it is time to write the story. Let's begin.

2
THE INCHOATE YEARS: 1940–1969

Inchoate: Not yet completed, lacking order

Some people reach focus early in life, others drift or bounce around, and still others never make it. I think of myself as a late bloomer, although by today's standards getting one's act together can take forever. I was born in a more privileged time, November 1, 1940 in the east end of Toronto at 14 Mallon Avenue. A Catholic as I was soon christened, born on 'All saints day', and named Michael (who is 'like god'). Not a bad start. Shortly after, although I have no memory of it, my father, Gerard, joined the Air Force and departed for the rapidly escalating Second World War. My mother, Mary Coffey, was a fine woman, skilled in sports, manager of our household, and destined to be a mother many times over.

The Early Years

My first five years as I mentioned earlier were idyllic. At the time Toronto was a sleepy urban sanctuary with little growth. In this solitude I was not only my mother's joy (pride came later, I hope) but was treasured by my mother's grandmother and aunts who lived very close by. I became increasingly connected with them as I moved into my euchre playing card days at age 6 and onward. In the midst of this dreamworld something happened. My father returned from the war and my parents started to produce a string of boys—Brian (1945), Rick (1946), Larry (1949), Ron (1953), Kevin (1955), and Dan (1957)—who will not figure much in this book as they were not connected to the ideas that we want to unearth given that these developed after I left home.

I have no idea what a 5-year old thought of all this commotion of men upon boys entering uninvited into his life, but I do remember that I invented an imaginary friend when I was about 5, named Jack. He became my constant playmate—hours and hours on end. We re-invented the world together. Maybe he was a substitute for my mother who was less and less available for me. At 3 years of age I called myself Bucky Bully—which evidently is how Michael Fullan sounds if you say it fast to a toddler. With a name like Bucky you can afford a little swagger. Looking back I wonder if being kicked off the pedestal at age 5 had a dramatic influence on my drive to be noticed, and have impact. I am only going to use three pictures in this book—the first at age 1 (Figure 1), the second at age 8 (Figure 2), and the third as a 12-year-old

Figure 1 Fullan age 1, 1941.

Source: the author.

Figure 2 Fullan age 8, 1948.

Source: the author.

Figure 3 Fullan age 12, 1952.

Source: the author.

hockey player (Figure 3). Here I am in Figure 1 as a budding bucky bully (is that a pedestal I am sitting on?).

As the need for a larger and larger house became evident we moved a few miles north, still in the east end to two houses in succession in the 1950s. From 1946–1953 I attended St. Brigid's elementary school, just north of Danforth Ave, where I did routinely well. Figure 2 shows me in grade 3—8 years old and ready to learn. I remember one teacher vividly, Sister Ste Leo Marie, because she taught me for three years running (grades 6, 7, and 8), made things interesting, and was cute. She said endearing things like "I am so inept when it comes to how things work that I am still surprised that the light comes on when I flip the switch". In addition, she taught me the basics well. My grades were usually about 75%, I skipped a grade and then went off to high school at the age of 12 (yes, 12; I was born at the time of year to start early and I skipped a grade). I attended St. Mike's High School—a private boys' school—in 1952, grade 9.

A slight diversion here: I won't dwell on my parents except to introduce them from time to time as I grew up. The basic thing to know is that their families of origin came from Ireland (Counties Clare, Kerry, Galway, and Tyrone –the latter eventually becoming part of Northern Ireland). In the 1800s the ancestors emigrated to Toronto and the surrounding area. We were what would be called a working class or lower class family. My father Gerry was gregarious and moved from career to career—a milkman who got up at 4am to deliver milk, an insurance salesman, a leading sports manager in hockey in the Toronto area including becoming manager of the famed St. Mike's Hockey Arena attached to the all-boys school that I attended. He was a great singer—an Irish tenor who once lost on a Buffalo-based television talent show to an 8-year-old girl who tap danced.

My mother was always the responsible one. I guess you could say that my father was in charge of generalities, and my mother in particularities. When it came to family finances, household management, day-to-day issues my mother was the detail person. With seven boys and little money I would have no hesitation in recommending her as Finance Minister.

My parents had two goals in mind for their boys: a university education, and hockey. I was to become the first person in our family—all uncles, aunts, and families included—to graduate from university. And all others would follow. We had a particular other powerful figure: my mother's father, Vince Coffey. Vince, my grandfather, was a formidable influence in my life. He had a grade 8 education and became a car and truck mechanic. He worked at Borden's Milk Dairy in Toronto (no connection as far as I know to my father's milkman days), and steadily worked his way up to become Manager of the entire fleet of Borden's trucks. Vince was tough, but was also the first man I knew that was genuinely emotional. When I was older, in my late 30s, I ended up at his house one evening having a nightcap with him (In his older age he always had one drink before going to bed). That night he pulled out a bottle of rum that he had just bought duty free on a trip. Unbeknownst to him and me it was 150 proof (drinkers will know that standard alcohol was 80 proof; 40% alcohol). We were drinking 75% alcohol! We had two or three drinks only to find that we ended up hugging each other, crying and expressing our love for each other. As I said he was emotional, but as a man he rarely showed it. I was not emotional but somehow the 150-proof rum was able to crack my code.

Vince had great basic values—live a good life, work hard, and, for the new generation, get a university education. As the first born among all the sons and daughters of aunts and uncles I was the first in line. He insisted that I go to university, and was to be instrumental later in this way when I started at University of Toronto. In early high school I was not aware that university was my destination—did not give it much thought. When I was about 15 years old I was working part time at the grocery store Loblaws, and one evening I said to my mother that I wanted to quit school and go to work full time at Loblaws. My mother said that I was too young, that she would have to sign for it, and she was not going to do that. I might have cried for 10 minutes, but nothing more came of it. Apparently I only thought about one day at a time — more empty-headed than anything.

My third picture (Figure 3) taken on April 17, 1952 by a Toronto newspaper shows me as a budding hockey player posing to tie the skates of a teammate. As the newspaper reported our team won the provincial championship and "Mike Fullan was the top star in the Toronto win as he netted two goals". The game was played at Maple Leaf Gardens, the iconic home of the Toronto Maple Leafs.

(Several of my younger brothers became better hockey players than me—three of them went to Cornell University on hockey scholarships and one, Larry, played in the National Hockey League (NHL) briefly.)

At the time I was about to enter grade 9 at St. Mike's College High School, age 12, joining an all-boys catholic high school. Six brothers, no sisters, and all male high school: my experience with girls continued to be abstract.

Another stroke of luck I had was in my first couple of weeks at school. A couple of older boys (everyone was older than me) started to pick on me and pushed me against the locker. I had a friend named Bobby Jones (a real friend, not like Jack) who was a few years older than me, from my neighborhood in the east end—and one maniacal tough guy—who happened by at the time. He took the older of the two boys and slammed him against the locker a couple of times, and said "if you every so much as glance at Mike again you are as good as dead". I never had any trouble from then on, and it was my first lesson in the importance of having teammates. Later, my forte as a leader was to build great teams around me who operated seamlessly with and without me.

In grades 9 and 10 I did well at school, but other things, like hockey and the associated camaraderie, were calling. St. Mike's school was located mid and uptown from where I lived, and when I first started attending there was not yet a subway line. Compounding this was my hockey that was beginning to kick in big time. There was a hockey rink in my area of town; Ted Reeves Arena by name. A group of eight or so of us discovered that we could rent an hour's worth of ice from 7–8am, and the night caretaker would let us come at 5am or so. Twice a week we began our day by showing up at the arena at five in the morning and playing hockey for two or three hours. We were spent (and often late) by the time we made the trek across town to school. Anytime there was a slight amount of snow we would declare ourselves late and go over to a local restaurant, called the Cottage, have coffee and drift into school at 9:30am or so. The school was administered and taught primarily by Basilian Fathers. The vice-principal was Fr. David Bauer, a decent hockey player in his own right. One morning he walked into the Cottage (I still remember his black leather gloves), surveyed the place, didn't use a notebook, and the next day called us by pairs into his office.

Our punishment was to administer five strap lashes to each hand, with each of us strapping the other. You can imagine the psychology. Another incident: in grade 10 we had a Brother (who shall remain nameless, but not to me) teaching us math. He was not a good teacher and was constantly under stress trying to control the class. He got mad one day at one of the boys, and berated him for not having graph paper. He shouted at the kid that all that was required was to go to the store to get the paper. And I chimed in, "and ten cents too". Brother X snapped and picked up a wooden pointer and smashed it over my head. Blood and five stitches later my parents came to the school with a minor complaint. No excessive physical punishment they warned, and nothing like that ever did recur. Shortly afterward, Brother X had a breakdown and left teaching.

My hockey bug was not helped by continuing to score a lot of goals, and by having Frank Mahovlich, and Gerry Cheevers—who went on to be superstars—in my grade 10 class. By the time I got to grade 12 (Ontario had 13 grades at that time) I was good enough for Junior B hockey, which was a step away from Junior A on the way to the NHL. Fr. Bauer was the coach and I scored a couple of goals in my first preseason game. I became noticed by the opposition, some of whom were as old as 20, and in the next few games they went after me—a 16-year-old. After observing a few hits Fr. Bauer counseled me out of Junior B. He must have remembered how I took to the strap.

The University Years

The next couple of years were uneventful as I approached the end of high school. I took two years to finish grade 13 which wasn't a bad thing given my very young age. I had a good education at St. Mike's, but not a great one, mainly through my own fault. I had few peers or family members who were strong scholars. The grade 13 provincial exams were tough and required for entrance to university. In my first attempt I failed a couple of exams and my parents sent me to summer school for makeup. The next year I completed my requirements, applied to university, and was accepted at St. Michael's College, University of Toronto. Yes, the first one in the greater extended family in all directions to enter university. My grandfather, Vince Coffey, paid my tuition in year one.

But it didn't register on me. I was, I have to say, being my inchoate self. I waltzed into university in 1959 with not much thought at all—age 19.

Year one at university, after attending a private catholic boys' school; all that freedom! If I had to give a label to my first year at university it would be 'the year of living irresponsibly'. I spent my time equally and fully at playing bridge, hockey, and beer drinking. I learned bridge in an odd way. A large group hung around the 'coup' (a sprawling lounge at our college) in between classes playing bridge. I watched day after day until one day somebody left for class and someone said to me "you play don't you, Fuller?" (we all had nicknames—some of the other ones I remember were Rip (I gave him the name because he slept a lot), bulldog (he had an enormous neck), stairs (because his hair cascaded upward from his forehead in perfect lateral tightly-knit waves), and pork chop (well, you can imagine)). I sat down and played bridge from that moment. I had never played before and never had instruction, but without skipping a beat I became a regular—hooked like a novice drug addict. Hockey was the inter-mural league within the different colleges within University of Toronto, and it was excellent hockey with lots of fans. Beer drinking was what we did every day, earlier and earlier it seemed.

Pretty soon for me there were no 'in between' classes. Shamefully, a handful of us competed in terms of how few classes we would attend. The whole year went by and I got to the point where I attended zero classes in the second term. In effect I unofficially dropped out without telling anybody. I had wasted my grandfather's tuition money without a thought.

I eventually told my parents that I had dropped out (never told the university), and I took a job in an insurance company in the summer of 1960. Three things happened in rapid succession in August. I was let go from the insurance job (they were cutting back); I received a letter from the university with my application for the coming year (this was strange as I had simply left without telling them and they were treating it as a normal application to continue in year one—no reference to my incomplete year, and no questions asked); the third was that a friend of my father's, Harry Walker by name, offered to pay my tuition if I went back to school. My father always had great friends but not much money, and Harry was one of his friends from the real estate business. I swear that I did not have any intention of returning to school, and I don't even think that my parents, let alone Harry, knew about my receiving the application to return. There may have been some behind the scenes conspiring that I was not aware of, but to this day I think that what happened was that it was August, that there was some general talk about me going back to university (which I never took seriously, not wanting to waste more time and money), and *on the same day* the letter from the university and offer from Harry came along. Surreal me returned to the university in 1960, year one of a three-year bachelor's degree.

I did what I had to do to get Bs and Cs. I passed year one. I had to pick a major for year two and selected Greek and Roman history for which I had a passing interest. I performed middling in years two and three ending with a bachelor's degree in the spring of 1963. I was an average student. One day an odd notion occurred to me for improving my education—or at least the trappings of it. I had noticed that my fellow students had a wider vocabulary than me. I was also fascinated by unusual words in the novels we were reading. Maybe I wasn't going to master the whole book I was reading, but I could improve my vocabulary. So I started a notebook where I wrote down alphabetically any new interesting word that I encountered followed by its definition. At first there is a tendency to go for words that you would never use, like parlous. My favorite was nugatory: meaning, of no value or importance, which is a bit ironic given the exercise. But I filled a whole book that ended up giving me a good vocabulary where I can now use words like pernicious when I need to (I still have this book of words).

In my second and third year I started to go with Sylvia, a fellow student who was in the field of science. We married in 1966 and I am afraid that I did not have much familiarity with girls and women. In my first five years of my life I had auditioned as a baby and child with my mother, great grandmother, and aunts and had done quite well. But then I had an all-boys immersion at home and at high school until age 18 that put me right out the picture in the girl department. I will tell you more about myself in this respect later.

As I finished my BA I have no doubt that my fellow students thought that I was an average student going nowhere. Most of my friends were from middle class families, and were heading to law, medicine, business, and so on. I was an ordinary student who was seen as not very serious about life.

Back to 1963. I had no idea what I wanted to do, and as a default I decided to apply for a master's program. I contemplated social work, and architecture but they seemed too specific. I decided on sociology—it was general enough, i.e. I did not have to commit to a particular field. To put all this another way, inertia carried me into graduate school. Once more I lucked out. My grades were not good (Bs and Cs) and I would not have been admitted to most departments or universities. But the field of sociology was just emerging in Canada and University of Toronto, and the university needed students as it began to build its department with some superstar faculty. I did not know this when I applied—really it was just a shot in the dark. I was admitted to the MA in September 1963 at the very time that the Department of Sociology was established as a spinoff from the Department of Political Economy. The great Canadian Samuel Delbert Clark founded the department—my first master's year, and the birth of the department were one and the same. Charles Tilly, a renowned sociologist and historian, taught me, and Jan Loubser, a young and upcoming sociologist from South Africa via Harvard, became my mentor and master's and doctoral supervisor.

Jan was fresh with his Ph.D from Harvard having studied with the famous Talcott Parsons. Professor Parsons was a structural function-alist who believed that social action was determined by one's values and structural conditions. The theory was that complex society functioned to promote stability over time. As a 'macro theory' it eventually had little appeal to me, because it was hard to understand and seemed to have no practical value (the latter eventually was what drove me). In particular, Parsons developed a four-fold framework organized around: adap-tation, goal attainment, integration, and pattern maintenance. This was followed by his five dichotomies that he called 'pattern variables': affectivity vs affective neutral; diffuseness vs specificity; universalism vs particularism; self vs collectivity; and achievement vs prescriptive. These five sets of dilemmas created 32 combinations. Need I say more?

In my master's I was steeped in structural functionalism, and studied the classical sociologists such as Max Weber and Emile Durkheim. The only reason that my experience was not deterministic was that the stuff was so damn hard to comprehend! I received straight As in all my courses, and somehow ended up doing my master's thesis on 'Unit autonomy in India'. I am currently searching the archives to find a copy of the thesis because I have no idea what the title means (presumably it has something to do with big centralized government with plenty of local freedom).

Completing my master's in 1963 with straight As, and nowhere to go, it was natural to enter the doctoral program. In a way this was inertia again. Straight As were rewarding, I had a mentor in Jan who wanted doctoral students, and so on. The path of least resistance claimed me. I worked more and more closely with Jan who garnered a large grant from the Canadian federal government to study worker alienation and the evolution of technology. As we started this work Jan was appointed chairperson of the newly created Sociology in Education department at the Ontario Institute for Studies in Education (OISE). OISE was established in 1965 by the Ontario government as a state of the art research-intensive institute with graduate programs in education. It was to be affiliated with University of Toronto for degree granting purposes, and had its own board of governors. The Sociology in Education department was established July 1, 1968 with Jan as its first chair of department. Jan hired me and three others as the first four faculty members of the department. I don't recall being interviewed for the job. It was more like Jan saying "I am going to accept the job as chair at OISE, do you want to join me as a faculty member?" I was hired as a lecturer (pending completion of my doctorate) at a salary of 12,000 CAD to commence at the same date the department opened: July 1, 1968. I had my first full time job, and by now two young children, Chris and Maureen, at 1 and 2 years of age.

Work at Last

The first year—a start up one—we had no students. This gave me the opportunity to finish my doctoral dissertation, which I did in time to formally defend it on November 5, 1969. This time, I do know what the title means: 'Workers receptivity to industrial change in different technological settings' (Fullan, 1969). I studied workers in four industries: printing, automobile, oil, and electrical equipment. My main five hypotheses were:

- Type of technology directly affects the degree of alienation from the job with alienation being highest among mass production workers (automobile) and lowest among continuous process (oil) workers.

- Type of technology affects certain structural conditions of organizations, which in turn influence the degree of integration of the worker in the organization with mass production workers being the least integrated and continuous process workers the most integrated.
- Alienation from the job is negatively related to the acceptance of industrial changes.
- Integration in the organization is positively related to the acceptance of industrial change.
- Alienation consisted of two components—powerlessness and meaninglessness. Integration was defined as: relationship with fellow workers, relationship with first line supervisor, labor-management relations, and the status structure of the organization.

By and large the hypotheses were confirmed, and I got my first taste of how relationships fared within organizations, and the growing presence of technology. I can't say the findings had much impact except for the large oil producing company that complained vociferously to Jan after our study that our survey was a catalyst for workers voting to become unionized! At this stage I was passively studying change. There was no notion in my mind that this would eventually become my life's work: namely that I wanted to help change things for the better.

I graduated from University of Toronto in 1969 as one of only three sociologists in the entire country of Canada. So there I was in 1969, beginning Assistant Professor scheduled to teach and do research in a graduate school of education having never taken a course in education in my life. Inchoate would be the word.

3

THE FORMATIVE YEARS: 1969–1988

Formative: Giving form or shape. Serving to form something, especially having a profound or lasting influence on a person's development

The next two decades—basically the 1970s and the 1980s—were a whirlwind of development for me and for the field of educational change (although I am aware that people have a tendency to declare that the most important periods of history are when they themselves lived). For me, I am going to call them: the *implementation* decade, and the *meaning* decade.

The Implementation Decade: The 1970s

I spent the decade—the 1970s—immersing myself in what was there about the phenomenon of change that intrigued me. The end of my Talcott Parson exposure was marked by my very first peer reviewed publication—'Education and adaptive capacity'—that I published with Jan Loubser in 1972 in the prestigious journal *Sociology in Education* (Fullan & Loubser, 1972). The idea was that social evolution, consisted of increased variation, and selective retention a là Darwin, and that both the quality of variation and the nature of retention were furthered by increased education. It really didn't mean much but it was good practice.

My new work had begun with my appointment to OISE in 1968— again a stroke of timing luck. The 1960s had been full of optimism and innovation in education: open plan schools, new math, team teaching, new curriculum in science and social studies. Then a series of studies began to appear: Goodlad et al. (1970), *Behind the classroom door,* Gross et al. (1971), *Implementing organizational innovations, and* Sarason (1971), *The culture of the school and the problem of change.* They all drew the same conclusion: innovations that were supposed to be the wave of the future were not being used as intended, and in any case there was no proof that they were in existence on the ground let alone put into practice. It was then that I made the distinction between adoption and implementation. The best analogy I could think of was when I was behind in my assignments or courses in graduate school I would go and buy a book or two that were relevant to my work, but I noticed belatedly that I wouldn't have to read the books to feel better. All I had to do was *buy* a relevant book! Purchasing the book was adoption, not reading it was failed implementation. You could feel that you were making progress just by buying the right books and seeing them on your shelf! One pair of evaluators, Charters & Jones (1973), called the phenomenon prosaically, "the neglect of the independent variable", but in plain English it can be called: "On the risk of appraising non-events". The problem was something was supposed to have happened; it didn't; and then evaluators came along to assess its impact. Hence, the issue of assessing a non-event.

As I digested these early and converging ideas I had my first idea:

Seminal Idea #1: Implementation is the sine qua non of educational change.

It seems simple now in retrospect, but the notion is that you can have all the ideas in the world, but if they don't get used they are not of much value. Of course this (no value in unused ideas) is not literally true. Politics are built on promises never fulfilled, but I was moving toward wanting to see and make a difference. As a seminal idea it was really not my idea. Goodlad, Gross, and Sarason had already identified the problem. But they were not seeing the implications of it as I was. I was soon to see it as a paradigm shift, which established my reputation as a new change theorist.

I always wonder about the fine line between plagiarism and originality. Certainly I am vulnerable to it, as I will mention from time to time, as much of my work is derivative. The best defense I have heard of plagiarism was the movie director at Cannes who was accused of plagiarism. After denying it, and then being shown the parallels to someone else's work, his defense was "my memory disguised itself as my imagination". I like to think that while I am indebted to the trio of books cited above that I did more with the concept of implementation than the authors did. My favorite, and he became my early mentor albeit mostly from a distance, was Seymour Sarason from Yale. Once I read *The culture of the school and the problem of change* I was hooked. From that day on I looked forward to and read every one of Sarason's books. Seymour was also a friend of OISE psychologist Dave Hunt, and used to visit OISE annually to give a lecture. I got to know him well and had many great exchanges (the only thing I didn't like about his work was that he never seemed to come up with ideas for solutions—a theme that increasingly preoccupied me as we shall see).

My first serious publication on the new theme was as editor of OISE's new journal called *Interchange*. The editor was Andy Effrat, who was one of the four of us hired as the first faculty members of the Sociology in Education department. He was slightly my senior, and wanted to give me a chance to edit a serious special issue on change. I was put in charge of V3, 1972, the special issue of *Interchange*. Here I published my first article on implementation under the title, 'Overview of the innovative process and the user'. I quoted Sarason as he analyzed the new math:

> As the new math developed the teachers knew two things that "a change was being discussed and contemplated, and that they, the teachers, were in on nothing".

(p.36)

Remember my reference in Chapter 1 to 'cognitive empathy'. Although I wasn't emotional about it, as I read Sarason, I could feel the plight of teachers being on the receiving end of someone else's ideas that not only disrupted their lives, but that would predictably lead to them being unfairly blamed for the failure of the ideas. I sensed that this was a theme that was going to be around for a long time, and that I had the fortune of being in on the ground floor.

In *Interchange* I wrote a 46-page introduction based on the somewhat linear model of 'effective change' that contained five elements: user objectives; adoption of sound innovations; users' acceptance; users' capabilities; effective outcome (Fullan, 1972). This formulation was almost totally on instinct since I had not yet done anything concrete on actual implementation.

Other favorable things happened to me. Jan Loubser, the chair of our department, was invited in 1968 by Norwegian sociologist Per Dalin to conduct studies of innovative schools and districts in Ontario as part of an international initiative that was called IMTEC (International Management and Training in Educational Change) that first began within the Organization for Economic Cooperation and Development (OECD). My part, with graduate student and soon to be friend Glenn Eastabrook, was to study an innovative school in the Toronto area. As an aside, and I can't verify that this is a fact for sure, this project took me on my first airplane flight ever—in 1968 to Norway, at the age of 28. Little did I know that drinking wine and writing books on airplanes and in airports would become a mainstay of my production. I spend a lot of time in airports and on planes.

The biggest advantage of the connection to IMTEC was being part of the birth of international studies of school improvement, and rubbing shoulders with the best consultants in the world. First there was Per Dalin, a bit of an arrogant, dynamic, intelligent, high energy, generous guy who was responsible for my global entry. I worked with him all through the 1970s as he broke with OECD. We had numerous events all around Europe that featured case studies of education in each country. Per was self-centered, which showed up in simple and complex ways. One simple and frequent example occurred when he was on the run (which was always). He would come back from a whirlwind trip wanting to have a team meeting that we all needed to catch up and plan. About half way through he would declare "I think we are all tired and we had better stop". Of course, he was the only one that was tired. More complex or annoying was when we carefully planned an important presentation. Being democratic in theory everyone would have a role to play such as kicking off an event. Per would sit in the front row and if he didn't think it was going well he would jump up and take over. But, he was very supportive, very generous with me, and in many ways was the father of international school improvement and his book *Limits to educational change* is a classic (Dalin, 1978). I lived in Oslo for most of one year (1975), along with at least 50 trips within Europe during the 1970s.

The bonus was that Per hired the best consultants in the world to work with us in the planning and running of conferences. The best, who became another mentor and close friend, was Matt Miles from New York. Matt was one of the founders of Organization Development (OD) and part of the human relations movement of organizational change. He was a trainer—the first one I worked closely with—and I learned a ton from Matt about learning design, group strategies, running workshops, and the like. This was to become a key part of our change strategies later—not only as a method of training, but also increasingly as a way of learning more from practitioners. Matt also taught me the discipline of hard work. Later we would do training consultancies with local school districts. After working all day we would go back to the hotel where I was looking forward to a relaxing meal and bottle of wine. Not so for Matt. He would insist that we spend a couple of hours with flip chart paper identifying the key lessons of the day, and planning the next day. We worked many years together, and I learned (first hand) that he was a fine gourmet—but only after the work was done.

With Per I also got to meet and know Milbrey McLaughlin from Stanford, who was at my stage of career. Milbrey went on to co-lead with Paul Berman the now landmark Rand, Change Agent Study (1973–1978), which helped define the field of implementation. While in Oslo I wrote (with graduate student Alan Pomfret) what we thought was and is the definitive review of research on implementation that we published in 1977 in the *Review of Educational Research*. Over 60 pages long and citing every study we could find, we analyzed and named the 'black box of implementation' as *the* central problem in school improvement.

Back in Toronto I teamed up with Glenn Eastabrook and we spent 1970–1977 in schools in Kingston, Ontario (where Glenn was based) and in Toronto observing in classrooms, and doing surveys of students and teachers, and case studies of schools. We learned a lot including themes that I would pursue the rest of my career. Just to name one set of findings about students:

A minority of students think that teachers understand their point of view, and the proportion decreases with educational level—41%, 33%, and 25% from elementary to junior high, and high school respectively.

Substantial percentages of students including one out of two high school students reported that "most of my classes or lessons are boring".

(Cited in Fullan, 1982, p.148)

Other things were happening. I showed an interest in leadership and was appointed chair of the Sociology in Education department from 1976–1981. I had a knack for it. I was fair, empathetic, and able to handle disagreements and conflict. Some of the arguments were theoretical which meant that they did not have much application, and thus were easy to contend with. I am sure I took the job for the wrong reasons (wanting to be important), but from those days forward I learned the most about leading change (and about myself) from the leadership positions that I held continuously from 1976 to the present. I learned a great deal from some of the leading feminists and critical theorists that we had on staff (Dorothy Smith, Mary O'Brien, and Margaret Eichler) in that small but powerful department in the late 1970s.

During this period my marriage with Sylvia was growing cold. I think I was a better father than husband, but anyway we separated and were divorced by 1979. It was drift more than decisive, and I was busy with my career. It was my fault and was part of the syndrome that I was afraid of personal commitment. I am not going to hop on the psychoanalyst's couch, but it can be said that personal commitments make me nervous. I have always found solace, engagement, and more success in my work. Not a great trait, but a fact.

The 1997 implementation article had given me high profile, and I was increasingly doing projects in the US at the Federal National Institute of Education, and some the federally administered research and development labs. The educational change movement had also started in the US in the mid to late 1960s. The first Federal education act was passed—the Elementary and Secondary School Act of 1965—that set out areas of programing and funding but without much strategy (in truth little was known about system change at the time). On one occasion in 1980 I was consulting with the Far West lab in San Francisco. I got on the plane to return home and found it half empty. I had been thinking of writing my first book (I was about to turn 40). On that plane and in an instant I had my second seminal idea that would carry me through and beyond the 1980s.

The Meaning Decade: 1980s

Seminal Idea #2: At the heart of educational change is personal and collective meaning.

My implementation work drove me deeper and deeper into the concepts of personal and collective meaning. Eventually it was to become the secret of change (and in my latest work, the secret of life for all learners). At this stage (1980) I wanted to map out 'meaning' in relation to every single role in the education system. As I spread out in an empty row for the 5-hour flight from San Francisco to Toronto, and thought about what would be my first major book it came to me that 'the *meaning* of educational change' was the breakthrough idea. For the next five hours I wrote non-stop naming each chapter, and writing a summary paragraph for each. The flight went by in a flash it seemed. The number and title of the 15 chapters did not change as I later wrote the draft. Six chapters in Part I, **Understanding Educational Change:** Purpose and plan of the book; Sources of educational change; The meaning of educational change; Causes and processes of adoption; Causes and processes of implementation; and Planning, doing, and coping with change. Part II, **Educational Change at the Local Level** also contained six chapters: The teacher; The principal; The student; The district administrator; The consultant; and The parent and the community. Part III, **Educational Change at the Regional and National Levels** had three chapters: Governments; Professional Preparation and Professional Development; and the Future of Educational Change.

I wrote most of it in the summer of 1981 and decided to send the manuscript to the most prestigious educational publisher I could think of: Routledge. Guess what? They rejected the manuscript observing that it sounded too much like Sarason! Latent plagiarism or what? On my second attempt Teachers College Press accepted the manuscript, and *The meaning of educational change* went on to be published in five editions (some under the title of *The new meaning of educational change*). The five editions appeared in 1982, 1991, 2001, 2007, and 2016b, selling a total of over 100,000 copies and served as a textbook in many college courses.

As I reflect on the sting (and compliment) of being too much like Sarason I feel vindicated in two ways. The first involved Seymour. Just as I finished my book Seymour was about to go to press with his second edition of *The culture of the school and the problem of change.* He had the generosity toward a rookie like me to stop the presses on his 1982 edition and enter the following footnote at the beginning of his book:

> After this book was put into the publication process, I read, thanks to Professor Michael Fullan ... a draft of his forthcoming book ... Fullan has written a most thoughtful and important book that, given its focus, is more comprehensive than mine in its analysis of discrete efforts at change. The two books are both overlapping and complementary in substance and conclusions.
>
> *(Sarason, 1982, p.4)*

Hmmm, when I reread his final sentence I sense that maybe he too thought that I had borrowed too much from him. But I was a beginner, and he was a star and wanted to help me out. Thank you, Seymour!

The second twist is ironic. The publisher who commissioned this book—the one you are holding in your hands or seeing on your screen—is none other than Routledge! Sometimes life can be appropriately long.

Something else was happening in 1980. I was about to marry my second wife, Wendy. We had met at OISE, had been going together, had bought a house and were living together in early 1980. On the morning of our wedding, September 10, 1980, I woke up and said to Wendy "I can't go through with it". I had been greatly troubled by how young my children were, and whether I was doing the right thing. Wendy was 28 and I was 40. She calmly said: "It is not practical to cancel it on the day. There are 150 people coming and everything is arranged". Wendy has great empathy—not just the cognitive kind, but the real McCoy, emotions and all. She knew that I was having a great deal of difficulty coming to a decision because of my children (or was it the real reason of failure to commit?). She pointed out that the guests had already got into their days and would show up at the church, and that I would look like a fool if I cancelled (not that this argument had any effect on me; when people are in a state of high anxiety, the last thing they think about is how it will look to others).

What we can do, Wendy continued, is that I, Wendy, promise that you can have a divorce anytime you want with no questions asked. I then said I am going for a walk which I did, had a cup of coffee and a donut (a Canadian tradition under all conditions), returned home and said okay, let's do it. (Later on Wendy told me that she took that stance not because she wanted me so desperately, but purely for practical reasons; too many people would be inconvenienced. It was the best way to solve the problem at hand. People who are emotionally grounded have such an advantage!).

We had a great wedding at Casa Loma in Toronto: my father sang Ave Maria that sent shivers down my spine; Wendy looked stunning; I was funny. And we lived happily ever after (mostly). We had our first child in 1983—a boy whom we named Bailey (in 1991 we had our second boy, Conor). Stemming from Wendy our whole family has become an oasis of mutual empathy—even I have picked up my game, cognitive with tears. I know the latter sounds a bit flippant, but believe me that I know my weaknesses in the emotional department.

My second marriage and the associated shenanigans with wanting to back out deserve 'seminal change recognition' in its own right. Yes, it's true that if you can think of a given change as not necessarily permanent you can cope with it better. That was Wendy's approach to a tough situation. Arising from this the real meaning for me is more basic. There is no meaning without action; or, if you prefer, if you want meaning take purposeful action.

Seminal Idea #3: All real change is action oriented.

I had been analyzing change for a decade and a half but couldn't apply it to myself—a not uncommon phenomenon in the professions. Emphasizing the personal took me beyond my cognitive empathy into the emotional zone where I had to be. Second, the seemingly innocent phrase 'action-oriented' has a lot more depth than it seems. From that day on and reinforced by other ideas that I will come to, I arrived at the view that you actually *learn best through action!* Wendy had been after me in other ways about my work observing: "you do great analysis but when are you going to get to solutions and help people?" I was already heading in that direction, but sometimes you need a push.

One of these practical avenues to action for me has been through the leadership positions I have held. Starting in 1976, as I mentioned earlier, I had become chair of the Sociology department—one of eight departments at OISE. In 1981 I became Assistant Director (Academic) at OISE—the second level from the top. My boss, the Director, was the brilliant Bernard Shapiro, and I was one of three Assistant Directors. I learned a lot from Bernard. On the positive side I learned the value of being decisive. After any good analysis Bernard had no trouble being direct and taking action with conviction. He also had unique insights like "I would rather pay a man to do nothing than to do the wrong thing"— when he wanted to move someone from a position where the person was not effective. His brilliance was sometimes a liability as when a government official we were working with confided in me: "The trouble with Bernard Shapiro is that he stops listening as soon as he has understood the point" (which says as much about the receiver of the message as it does about Bernard). In any case I learned a lot about leadership and change in the six years I held the post (1981–1987).

We will return shortly to my 'administrator as learner' role, but first, much also was happening with my change ideas in the 1980s. I was already part and parcel of the new implementation and dissemination crowd: Milbrey McLaughlin and Paul Berman of the famous RAND Change Agent studies, Judith Warren Little on staff development and collaboration, David Crandall, Karen Seashore Louis, Matt Miles, Michael Huberman, and others of the large-scale DESSI (Dissemination Efforts Supporting School Improvement) research, and so on. So, I was pretty plugged in to the new implementation decade and was a leader myself within the movement. On the bigger scene was US President Reagan's federal commission in education that released its report, *A nation at risk* (1983), with its famous characterization of the public education as system as 'a rising tide of mediocrity'. But alas it contained no remedies.

In 1987, Noel Clark, the Executive Director of the Ontario Public Schools Teacher Federation (OPSTF, the teachers' elementary school union), came to me with an offer in which he said: School principals (members of our federation) are complaining that the job is getting worse, more and more overloaded, and becoming impossible to handle. What we would like, said Noel, is for you to write a booklet that will help them. We will give you the title and three criteria: the title is *What's worth fighting for in the principalship* (WWFFP), and the criteria are: Write something that is: i) deeply insightful, ii) make sure it contains lots of practical-action advice, and iii) above all make it concise. I told Noel that he could have any two of the three; but more seriously I took it on because it was exactly the direction I wanted to go in: now that I knew a great deal about change, I said to myself, why not try to be deliberately helpful. Little did I know that this would open up a whole new rich vein of learning.

This WWFFP booklet published in 1988 became enormously popular among principals and others. I had made myself write in a new way, and it had worked. All my future writing has been influenced by that shift to conciseness and action-helpful. The biggest and most satisfying compliments that I get are things like: "it is as if you were in my shoes", "I followed your advice and am getting great results: you have changed my life". It wasn't just what I said but that I had said it in a way that people were able to build on with their own ideas.

Another fortuitous happening: in my academic Assistant Director role I was responsible for negotiating contracts in the hiring of all new academics to OISE. One such person was Andy Hargreaves who at the time was a 36-year-old sociologist in England. I gathered the references, and one such letter in a typically straightforward English manner said, Andy is a brilliant young sociologist, but he is raw. I can't remember if the referee used the term stroppy, but I got that meaning. He went on to say that Andy would be worth every annoyance as he will only develop and develop to become a superstar.

We hired Andy, and I must say that part of the reason was selfish on my part because I admired his emerging work on collaboration. He had not yet formed his new insights, but was hot on the trail to do so. His initial work when he came to OISE began to flesh out these ideas: contrived collegiality, balkanization, and the like. OPSTF wanted more work on the concept of 'What's worth fighting for' and we agreed on two more books to complete a trilogy; for these Andy and I would work together. Andy and I then wrote, *What's worth fighting for in your school* (WWFYS), and a bit later, *What's worth fighting for out there* (1992 and 1998, respectively). Andy is a deeper and more innovative thinker than I am, and I was more applied and practical at the time. We helped each other strengthen our strengths, and become more like the other in terms of addressing our mutual weaknesses, although from the beginning Andy had a penchant for application, which he demonstrated when we did the 'action guidelines' for WWFYS. We eventually did our own share of fighting, but that is another decade and another story that we will come to, and is germane to the evolution of my change ideas, and my own personal and professional development.

One final relevant development in the 1980s pertains to my Assistant Director, Academic role. OISE was independent with its own board of governors but did not have degree granting authority. For the latter it depended on recurring five-year agreements with the University of Toronto. We at OISE assumed that they would be automatic into perpetuity as they had been since the inception in 1965. The university, for reasons I will come to, were not so satisfied with the status quo. They had a large faculty of education (called FEUT, Faculty of Education, University of Toronto) that was engaged primarily in pre-service and in-service education, but was not seen as a scholarly institution, which greatly disturbed the university (even though the university had not made any investment toward that end). In the early 1980s the university and OISE formed a 'Joint Council in Education' (JCE) to explore and develop relations between OISE and FEUT. I was the main OISE representative and we spent a couple of years getting to know each other —at least the members of the JCE. But none of us on the FEUT or OISE side had any intention of merging.

The University of Toronto, however, had two reasons for wanting a change. One was that FEUT was badly in need of development and they, the university, did not want to take that on. The university had treated FEUT for years as a cash cow. It was a big cow—some 120 tenure stream faculty with 1300 teacher education students, and thousands of part time in-service students. The university wanted to merge OISE and FEUT, which in effect would have OISE run the new faculty. The second reason, led by the Provost and the Dean of the Graduate schools, was that University of Toronto saw OISE as having pockets of weak standards with respect to admissions, and doctoral dissertations (and furthermore it was very large making up almost one quarter of the entire graduate school). OISE faculty and its Board of Governors would have no part of such a merger discussion with FEUT and University of Toronto, so it never even got to the table at that point.

At the time—1987—University of Toronto did not want to go to the wall on the matter because any arrangement would have required

Ontario Government approval and it seemed that the timing for such conflict was not right. But the university was facing a problem. The term of the current Dean at FEUT was soon to expire, and there were a large number of faculty retirements on the horizon. FEUT had been allowed to flounder with no (and I mean zero) new faculty appointments for at least a decade. The decision facing them was to close the faculty or appoint a new Dean with a mandate for renewal.

Somehow, in the same time frame Michael Connelly, a respected professor at OISE, and I were commissioned by a government Ontario Teacher Education Review Steering Committee to carry out a review of teacher education for the province. We completed our report in January 1987 under the title, *Teacher education in Ontario: Current practice and options for the future* (Fullan & Connelly, 1987). We were on good terms with the Dean of FEUT, John McDonald, and he invited us to present our findings to an FEUT faculty meeting. They were in none too good a mood to hear the theoretical generalities from a couple of Professors who had never taught pre-service teachers. The event went off without a hitch and after the meeting as we were leaving I overheard one of the veteran English professors (who was very English himself) say to Dean McDonald, "will these chaps be back"?

It turned out that one of these chaps would be back as the Dean's search committee for John McDonald's replacement approached me in the spring of 1987 to inquire whether I would please meet with them. I don't think that it was our report that caught their attention but rather several of the University of Toronto leaders had gotten to know me through the JCE, and they knew I was a solid scholar.

I met with the search committee, and we had a mutual size up. I had learned to be a straight talker from Bernard Shapiro and eventually said that I would be interested, but only if they were serious about developing FEUT. They said they were and sent the Assistant Provost to negotiate with me. I knew that there were a slew of early retirements coming up at FEUT (we estimated 22 FTEs as we call them—full-time equivalents). The Assistant Provost and I agreed that the FEUT budget would stay intact for the next three years, and that I as Dean would be able to retain the budget for the 22 positions subject only to the usual procedure of getting given positions and nominees approved. The entire budget would be mine to manage. Those of you who know universities know how incredibly unusual such an arrangement is. But the Shapiro in me pulled it off: I argued that giving me three years of money that is already in the budget is a small price to pay compared to 20 years of ripping off the faculty as a cash cow. There was no acrimony and the university agreed. I signed a contract in the spring of 1987 to start as the new Dean of FEUT beginning February 1, 1988. There were to be a few months to catch my breath, and then a challenge of unknown proportions. If I wanted action, I was going to get it in spades.

4
THE BECOMING YEARS: 1988–2003

Becoming: To come into existence; to undergo change or development

With *What's worth fighting for* I was in a new mode of applied action. Now being Dean of a faculty that badly need renewal I had no choice: action was essential. Here is the next seminal idea that I had already learned.

> *Seminal Idea #4: Be as assertive as you can get away with; including the kicker, but only if they thank you afterward.*

I had been preparing for this role for 20 years, and now had the opportunity to really learn. One of the biggest lessons that I cherished from here on in is 'always surround yourself with a great team, give them leeway, help them learn from each other, and learn from them yourself'. This 15-year era covers two Deanships both representing big change. I led two big transformations, but increasingly as we get to the end of this chapter I wanted to help lead substantial change in the educational world—not out of arrogance but because that was where moral purpose and making an impact converged.

The Faculty of Education FEUT, 1988–1996

I was appointed to the Deanship in the spring of 1987, and took up the position as of February 1, 1988. I knew two things as I headed for this role. One, Anne Millar the Associate Dean of FEUT, was a gem. Able to see the big picture, was flexible as required, well respected, incredibly committed and hardworking, and was superb at detail. Eventually at her retirement I praised her for being like the famed Czech hockey goalie, Dominik Hasek (you couldn't get anything by her). Anne and I were the perfect complementary team. We both wanted fundamental change to a faculty that had become moribund. She had local knowledge, and was an expert at detail. I had the big picture and the political and professional connections. And we liked each other. I appointed Anne as Associate Dean and we were off to the races. Another vital team member who would become my personal administrative savior for the next 15 years was Mary Stager who joined me from OISE as my executive right hand person. A third was Marnie de Pencier who was a fabulous policy person. Nancy Watson my chief researcher also joined me. There were more, but the point is that great teams have been the secret to my success since 1988.

At our first faculty meeting in February, 1988 I faced the 84 faculty members with a mandate for renewal in my back pocket—84 professors who had been at FEUT for a minimum of a decade and a half: yes, I was the first new appointment in 14 years! The challenge was to move fast and gain each other's respect. I had already decided in consultation with Anne that I would announce a new Learning Consortium on day one, February 1, 1988. It consisted of four school districts in the Toronto area (at the time North York, Scarborough, Halton, and Dufferin-Peel Catholic districts), OISE (I still had friends there), and FEUT. Each member put in 20K as an annual membership. Joanne Quinn, the superintendent of curriculum of Halton, who was their rep told me later that when she reported back to her Director, Bob Williams, she said, "I don't know what the hell it is but we can't miss it—I need 20K".

Much of the research in the 'implementation' and 'meaning' decades was about individual school experiences. I wanted to shift our interest to include the *system level*—in this case the district. The idea was that the universities (OISE and FEUT) would be in the business of school and district improvement, and that the districts would be in the business of teacher education and professional development. In fact, in many ways 1988 is a watershed year in the study of educational change in that the role of the district was introduced more explicitly. There had been references to district administrators but not to districts as systems. We appointed

Nancy Watson as the first executive director of the Learning Consortium. Nancy has been a career-long chief researcher in most of my endeavors—brilliant, loyal, hard working; never suffered fools gladly (except for the many times she was tolerant about my shortcomings).

I don't want to divert into a full-scale case study of FEUT but I do want to identify the change highlights. In the first 17 months (February 1, 1988 to July 1, 1989) we had 22 faculty positions to fill (due to regular and early retirements). I chaired every search committee (about five people with representatives from the home department and elsewhere). We had three equal criteria: a person comfortable working with practitioners, including being a good teacher; good at and committed to research; and being a good team member and collaborator. We spent the next five years stocking the faculty with these newcomers.

At the same time there were many of the incumbent faculty who wanted change: David Booth, Keith Mcleod, and several others. They were a proud group who had been mistreated badly by the university; most were not researchers; many were absolutely outstanding teachers; and there were several whose time had past. I learned the hard way in a couple of cases not to write off people who appeared different than myself. In one case I ended up having to give a veteran professor a huge payout because I had insulted him implying that we no longer needed him. I learned a lesson—treat people with dignity and appreciate the contribution they might have made under other circumstances.

The first summer (1988) we held a summer institute through the Learning Consortium that was based on 'cooperative learning' teaching that brought together over 150 teachers and administrators from the four districts; six veteran FEUT faculty members (all of them were veterans by definition) attended voluntarily (as one said to me later, I wanted to find out what the hell was going on before it was imposed on me).

The Learning Consortium development contains several key change lessons. First, as a change strategy it has all the trappings of one that is closely akin to *Seminal Idea #3 (All real change is action oriented)*, namely, *Ready, fire, aim.* When a situation desperately calls for change don't take a year to study the problem. Have a good directional idea (ready), get to purposeful action quickly (fire), learn from the action and consolidate (aim). We are also into new territory that involved mixing academics and practitioners who had little previous cultural experience working with each other. We started down this path in a hurry. My term commenced February 1, 1988. The first summer institute with 200 practitioners and faculty was to be held in July 1988—precious little time to plan.

One extremely favorable factor concerned the leadership of the institutions that joined. We were all professional friends and part of a study group consisting mainly of newly appointed Directors (District Superintendents) that met informally on Friday nights about four or five times a year: Veronica Lacey, North York (this was before the school board re-structuring that took place in the last part of the 1990s), Bob Williams, Halton, and Pauline Laing, Durham (the fourth district, Dufferin-Peel Catholic was not part of our informal group). The representatives that formed the steering committee were also young leaders on the move: Joanne Quinn from Halton (who now works with me in key roles), John Plumpton (an avid member of the International Churchill Society) from North York, Norm Green from Durham who was a dynamic, irrepressible staff developer and, Denis Thiessen from FEUT, one of the great new faculty members that I had hired, and Andy Hargreaves soon participated as an OISE rep.

Still, we were two different cultures (the field and the university), and in reality three cultures as OISE and FEUT were very different. In March we had our first meeting to plan the summer institute that we had decided should be on peer coaching and cooperative learning. We had invited to the meeting the international expert and peer coaching guru Bruce Joyce to help lead the summer institute. I knew Bruce, and as I mention later he had already tipped me off to hire Carol Rolheiser and Barrie Bennett of Edmonton as new FEUT faculty members; both had recently completed their doctorates in cooperative learning with Bruce and Beverly Showers at the University of Oregon.

Bruce Joyce is brilliant, and he and Beverly were pioneers in peer coaching, staff development, and instruction. He can also be prickly—arbitrarily so. One of the field reps happened to say: "we are so excited to have you here and to be doing a summer institute in peer coaching". Bruce took exception and gruffly said "we don't do peer coaching". There was a stunned silence (the point he wanted to make was peer coaching is only a means to an end—the end being improved student achievement). Everything went off the rails from there and by the time we adjourned there were at least two representatives who said, "we can't have Bruce Joyce do the summer institute". I will relate another Bruce Joyce story in a moment, but to finish this one, we checked out Carol and Barrie and found that they had fantastic reputations as instructors (they were indeed teachers' teachers). The two of them led the summer institute, which turned out to be an incredible success. Every single person loved it including a half dozen veteran FEUT faculty members who attended as participants. We were off to a great start.

The Learning Consortium also surfaced a perennial (and healthy) tension between research and practice. Those who want to change practice in a hurry (me included) sometimes often don't stop to take into account all the research, or may draw conclusions too quickly. On the other hand, bona fide researchers may be too slow to act until they get more facts (a kind of ready-ready-ready). As I said, a healthy tension to have if the two groups interact as they did in the Learning Consortium. In this case, Dennis Thiessen (one of the great new hires we had made at FEUT) pushed the consortium to be more critical. Yes, everyone was happy, but what was the impact? One of Andy's graduate student's, Ruth Dawe, did an evaluation that found that much of the training wasn't being implemented because it wasn't supported by the culture of the school. Andy got involved and began to show the applied side of his development by recommending that training include the development of collaborative cultures. Norm Green did a 180-degree turn and insisted on more research on impact. All in all the Learning Consortium represented a massive learning curve for all of us in bringing out the researcher in the practitioner and vice versa.

Back to Bruce Joyce: he and I met from time to time, and around this period we got together at my house over a couple of Scotches. I was interested in how good ideas can get better implemented. I knew that he and Beverly's model—theory, demonstration, practice, feedback, and coaching—was powerfully effective so I pushed him on what his 'theory of action' was on getting people to adopt the model. He didn't seem to understand the question: to him the model *was* the theory of action. It reminded me of the scene in *Get Smart* where the chief said to Max, "this mission is extremely dangerous, you could get captured and it could be deadly". The chief said, "I am going to give you this pill which when ingested causes instant death". Max then said, but chief how do I get them to take it? In Bruce's case the pill (the model) was good, but for me the problem remained 'how do we get them to take it?' Push upon push with Bruce finally got an exasperated response from him: you want my theory of action—it's *candor* he replied dramatically! Candor—being right—of course is not a complete theory of action, but later on we will see that candor is indeed part of the solution. Hint: solutions need precision (candor supplies that), but they also need motivation to act. Also, precision is not prescription, so there needs to be a degree of voluntarism. Stay tuned.

Shortly after the beginning of my term as Dean my grandfather, Vince, whose $400 I had wasted, but whose dreams for me were beginning to be realized, died in 1989 at age 96. I still consider him to be one of the great inspirations in my life.

Overall I learned several lessons as Dean of FEUT. First, when you are bringing about fundamental change, don't expect many compliments in the first three years. Second, involve people in shaping the new direction while being firm that there must be a new direction. Third, don't pigeon hole people. They may be behaving the way they are because of the circumstances. Change the setting and many of the people will change in surprising ways (many of the most respected veterans became champions of the new FEUT, and served as mentors to their younger new colleagues). Fourth, treat people with dignity. There are good and bad ways to leave a place or retire. One of the ways that worked for us was that the university had an attractive early retirement plan, and most FEUT faculty were on the Ontario Teachers' Pension plan which was also solid. I arranged multiple retirements where faculty members retired from their tenure stream position, and I hired them back on a lesser salary on a half time basis for one, two, or three years. It was as if they hadn't left. FEUT saved money, soon had access to a tenure stream position, and individuals were well off financially—money wasn't the issue; pride was. The fifth and final thing I learned about myself was a negative. I did not spend enough time with people when it came to their concerns—personal or professional. I did the big things right; I selected, built, and spent time with the team; I listened well when I was there; I had cognitive empathy and addressed problems from that perspective, and I was seemingly a nice guy. But I did not emotionally engage enough. I was selfish in wanting to pursue my own academic interests. Thank God I had Anne and other members of the team.

Be that as it may, FEUT got a new life and a growing reputation for research (for the first time large numbers of faculty presented at professional conferences like the Canadian Society for Studies in Education (CSSE) and the American Education Research Association (AERA)), greater presence in schools through the Learning Consortium, and increased reputation for good teaching. I should also add that FEUT was responsible for and housed a grade 7–12 school called UTS (University of Toronto Schools), which is a diverse, high performing school that has been in operation since 1908. The history of UTS warrants a book in its own right.

FEUT's new success notwithstanding, FEUT and OISE were no closer, and the university was getting increasingly impatient about wanting integration for both what I would call positive reasons (to have a world class school of education that combines and integrates teacher education and graduate programs), and negative reasons (take greater control of graduate school standards). It was 1994 and getting close to re-negotiating the University of Toronto/OISE affiliation agreement.

But this time the conditions were different. Rob Prichard, who had been Dean of the Law school when I first became Dean of FEUT (so we knew and supported each other), had been appointed President of University of Toronto at the age of 40—a dynamic, aggressive change agent in his own right. The Provost, Adela Sedra, an engineer by trade, became a good friend and supporter of education. Charles Pascal, who had been a department chairperson at OISE when I was chair of sociology, had become Deputy Minister of Education. One of my former colleagues at OISE, Angela Hildyard, had become Director of OISE. If any changes were to be made it would require a complicated tri-partite negotiation among Rob and the university Board of Governors (and me as Dean), Angela and the OISE Board of Governors, and the Ontario Government represented by Charles as Deputy Minister.

A whole book could be written on the merger of OISE and University of Toronto with the government's legal agreement. I can only give the highlights here. The initial trigger for aggressively exploring the merger came from OISE Director Arthur Kruger who in 1994 went to Charles Pascal, who was Deputy Minister, and said that a merger was needed because of OISE's financial situation. Pascal convinced his

Minister of Education (Dave Cooke, New Democratic Party (NDP) that was in power at the time) to raise the merger idea with Kruger, and Rob Prichard, the President of University of Toronto, and me as Dean of FEUT. When all agreed to pursue the merger, Kruger resigned and was replaced by Angela Hildyard who came in as acting Director of OISE. When the process to merge was announced anxiety went sky-high. FEUT faculty were nervous that OISE with their greater size and academic caliber would swamp them; OISE faculty were worried that the merger would result in being swallowed up by University of Toronto. Given the size and the complexity, and the nod to deciding things democratically it represented an enormous challenge. One saving grace was that we had built up FEUT (with several of the young faculty being graduates from OISE) so that it represented a reasonably attractive partner: FEUT had become, in a word, more integratable.

With the government's leadership and endorsement we established a joint OISE/University of Toronto negotiating committee with oversight by Charles to ensure fairness and legislative support. For many months talks went at a snail's pace, rumors swirled. We soon got to the stage of requiring a mediator. Charles appointed John Stubbs, President of Simon Fraser University. There was great resolve on the part of Rob Prichard to get a deal because he knew that a high quality school of education was essential for the future. Rob taught me the most about deep cognitive empathy. In my change work I derived my own insight that I called 'impressive empathy' which I defined as having empathy for people who are in your way (that's why it is impressive!). Empathy is 'understanding where people are coming from as if you were in their shoes'. It is not necessarily agreeing with them, but rather it is understanding them deeply enough that you have a chance of figuring out what might meet their needs. Indeed, it might involve thinking of a novel solution that the other side had not thought about but that addresses a concern or goal. Rob was good at this kind of negotiating. He was also known as an inveterate self-promoter of anything to do with University of Toronto. He had what we might call practical and political empathy: how can we find a different and better ground for meeting our mutual interests?

The sessions became more frequent and longer, alternating between direct face-to-face talks and internal team retreats in a local hotel. One night as we got down to details, Rob was briefing Charles Pascal by telephone, and as usual Rob's proposal included making a strong and aggressive pitch for a particular part of 'the deal' that favored University of Toronto. The rest of our team including me was standing around broadly listening in. The conversation became more and more heated with Rob saying "Charles, we already agreed on that point three days ago". Charles apparently did not agree, and Rob, knowing that Charles and I were friends, handed me the phone suddenly and said: "here, you talk to him". I started in, "Chuck, we already came to agreement on that point" whereupon Chuck said, "Fuck off" and slammed down the phone. So much for my persuasiveness, let alone my negotiating skills. I kept talking for another 15 seconds pretending that Chuck was still on the line, so that Rob and the team did not know that I had been rejected so dramatically. However, I did know the players and assumed that we would work it out, so I didn't take the re-buff personally.

We did finally reach agreement in the spring of 1995 in a marathon session that went back and forth non-stop from a Thursday afternoon to 5am Sunday. I remember leaving the hotel room at 6am on a dead quiet, peaceful Sunday morning in downtown Toronto. It felt like a great, and yes, surreal day. We had agreed on a number of key clauses that included earmarking for three years all the administrative money that would be saved (over ten million annually to be at the disposal of the new Dean), and other conflict resolution clauses that diverted disagreements into problem solving mechanisms. Still, both sides were wary of being swallowed up by the other group. The new integrated faculty was scheduled for official opening July 1, 1996 in order to give enough time for the transition and the appointment of a new Dean for what was to be called OISE/UT (not at all imaginative but we had bigger fish to fry).

There is a precarious footnote to the merger. Once the agreement had been reached between the two parties, and by the government (but before it went to Cabinet for approval) there was an election and Mike Harris, Conservative Party, became Premier. After a briefing between the new Minister, John Snobolen, and Charles as Deputy, about 'the deal' Snobolen said, "The Premier's Office is interested in closing OISE to make a point about austerity. What reasons can I use to keep it open? What will this new entity do for my friends who have children aged 4, 8, and 14?" to which Charles replied, for the 14-year-old, not much, but if this new OISE is successful we will have the best of world class scholarship informing quality teaching in the classroom. Snobolen then replied, "Fine but to achieve this will require a transformational leader who knows how to bring two cultures together. Do you know who it will be?" Chuck responded: "Yes, but it is confidential, but I can tell you the first Dean is one of the world's best at this" (thus more than compensating for telling me to fuck off). (The above paragraph is based on notes from Charles Pascal, July, 1995.)

If you believe that the merger of OISE and University of Toronto/ FEUT has been a good thing the heroes here are: Charles Pascal, who argued successfully by convincing Minister Snobelen to keep OISE from the chopping block, and the key roles played throughout the process by Angela, Chuck, Rob, me, along with surprising heroics on the part of the eventual education villain, John Snobelen (Snobelen went on to slash the education budget and along with Mike Harris became arch enemies of education and of the teachers).

In late spring, 1995, the university/OISE search committee recommended Michael Fullan for the position of Dean, which the university accepted. I had a year to focus on the transition with my official start date, July 1, 1996 for the regular seven-year term to end in 2003.

Before I turn to the next exciting chapter in my professional life I feel the need to give an update on my change thinking and activity. Of course being Dean of FEUT at a tumultuous time was a laboratory for learning about real change. I wanted to adapt Lewin's observation 'if you want to understand something, try changing it' to a more direct one: 'if you want to understand change, try changing something big'. I became a firm believer, as I am today, that you learn the most through purposeful doing. The best crucible for learning about change is the 'action-pit'.

A surprising bonus I got from my time at FEUT was my shift from being an academic lecturer to a workshop leader. Because we were committed to improving teaching we hired some excellent new pedagogues. Shortly after the announcement of my appointment as Dean, Bruce Joyce, as I noted above, contacted me and said that if you are looking for great new, young faculty that he had two doctoral graduates from Edmonton who would be ideal. In a flash I hired Carol Rolheiser to the faculty, and Barrie Bennett to the Learning Consortium (and later to the faculty). We started immediately in the summer of 1996 to do institutes on cooperative learning and change, and haven't stopped since. Carol, Barrie, Joanne Quinn, Norm Green, and others started to convert me from a stand up lecturer (and not a good one at that) to a workshop leader (which made me a better stand up speaker to boot). I don't know how long it took them to train me before I was allowed to lead my own workshop, but I think it is accurate to say that I am now an accomplished trainer. Designing and leading workshops is an excellent way to learn, learn, and learn.

While I was immersed at FEUT I did produce the second edition of *The meaning of educational change* (1991). I also wrote a new theoretical book called *Change forces: Probing the depths of education reform* (1993). There I set out in theoretical form the main themes that were crystalizing for me: moral purpose and change agentry; the complexity of the change process; the school as a learning organization; the learning organization and its environment; teacher education: society's missed opportunity; and the individual and the learning society. I was ready for more.

OISE/UT: 1996–2003

Having been at both FEUT and OISE, and now with the job of integrating the two into a new smooth entity, I felt like someone riding two Trojan horses into battle (at least I was transparent about it). Again I had the team: Mary Stager as my chief assistant, Ken Burke from the university became head of finance, and personnel. The three Associate Deans were Anne Millar, Angela Hildyard, and respected international scholar Ruth Hayhoe as head of research. They all worked seamlessly with me, and with each other. I knew how to select people, and how important it was to give them autonomy with the expectation that they work together and draw on me as required. Later as we needed replacements we hired Carol Rolheiser as Associate Dean Pre-service (Carol is currently (2017) head of the faculty development unit for all of University of Toronto—a huge responsibility). Ken Leithwood, a great researcher on leadership, but also a first rate administrator, eventually became Associate Dean, research. He helped me tremendously in relating to the university. I developed an insight that was a positive derivative of Ronald Reagan's observation. When he was dealing with Gorbachev he made the point that he had to 'trust and verify' (because he did not trust him). The team related version is *trust and interact* because if there is continuous interaction you do get to resolve issues more naturally in the day-to-day culture. You do get to appreciate each other's strengths (and limits), and you sooner than later gel as a team. This is how a team builds rapport—through getting to know each other through purposeful transactions. Thus, creating a new culture of interaction and respect is the key.

> *Seminal Idea #5: A leader is only as good as the team she/he builds and interacts with. Trust and interact is the key to mutual efficacy.*

The merger represented a massive agenda. It had all the change ingredients imaginable. Two large faculties totaling some 180 professors; multiple sets of overlapping unions; two different cultures (FEUT's pre-service teaching with a somewhat more formal university tradition; OISE more democratic and informal with its graduate studies' sense of entitlement); two different structures: OISE with eight departments, and FEUT with seven or so; and the ultimate change test in a university: who gets what office.

For the next four years in particular we went about addressing the problems. We resolved the labor union differences. Early on the department chairs of both faculties met informally without me and then proposed that integration could be addressed through a series of cross appointments without any structural changes to the status quo. I said a flat no because keeping the existing structure would have little chance of changing the culture. We went back to the drawing board and did forge an acceptable structural set of new departments where faculty members from both former institutions intermingled. We worked hard at appointing key leaders (chairs of the new departments for example); and I used the ten million dollar transition fund to buy people out who no longer wanted to be there or who did not fit. All in all it was a fairly smooth and successful transition by all counts. As Dean I was also blessed with having two of the greatest political champions of public education on my Advisory Board of trustees at OISE/UT—William Davis, former Premier of Ontario, and founder of OISE, and John Evans, former President of the University of Toronto. They were outspoken advocates of the vision of OISE/UT and supported me substantially, especially in my first term as Dean in the late 1990s.

By the time we got to year five—the year 2000—things began to change. Rob Prichard and Adel Sedra had left. I was due for a six-month sabbatical which I took. For the final two and a half years in my term as Dean I felt increasingly less connected to the university as a whole. The place ran well because I had a fantastic team. The new Provost was old-style academic, and we did not get along. At the best of times I did not like or feel comfortable in the traditional university style of meetings of Deans and Chairs, and the broader university culture where there seemed to be an enormous amount of abstract talk. I spent less and less time at university meetings, and was less fully present within OISE/UT, although the fact that we had such a good team who made best decisions with and without me made the problem less obvious. I knew a lot about leadership and effective organizations and felt increasingly that not being present enough was my Achilles heel.

Nothing went wrong (although I feel it could have been better), and people have continued to assure me to this day that they appreciated my style and substance, and would not have wished for any change. Still, I know that it was not ideal in moving to the next phase of development for the institution. I left the Deanship quietly in June 2003, and retired from the university as Professor Emeritus. As I departed in 2002–2003 the phenomenon of system change in the education world was heating up, and I was poised to become a key member of the global community of scholars and doers.

Counting my undergraduate years I had spent 45 years at University of Toronto. I am still part of the university and despite what I said about abstract talk, it gave me my intellectual and practical life for which I am eternally indebted. University of Toronto is routinely the number one or two ranked university in Canada. In OISE/UT, the University had embraced and developed one of the top faculties of education in the world.

5

The System Years Part One: 2003–2013

System: An assemblage or combination of things forming a complex whole

It was the allure of big change, and major consultancies with large education systems that took me away from university administration, and this gets us back to the change themes as they evolved over my 50 years. We have seen that adoption (developing innovations) characterized the 1960s; failed implementation the 1970s; and small-scale change in the 1980s. *A nation at risk* appeared in 1983 with frightening rhetoric and no remedies as the education system tried to move ahead with ad hoc innovations at the school level. At the end of the 1980s and into the 1990s we began to see some action at the district level: Elmore's district two from New York City, and our own Learning Consortium. Then starting in 1997 two newer and bigger things began to draw me in. One positive, and one negative, and I became hooked for good on system change.

First, the positive learning experience. In 1997 Tony Blair was elected to his first term. He appointed Michael Barber as his chief education strategist and they set up an implementation unit that Michael led. I had known Michael only passingly prior to this and was intrigued by the aspirations. The goal was to transform the entire primary school system in England in order to improve literacy and numeracy in all 20,000+ primary schools. Blair was quoted as saying "we are going to use the change knowledge to get there". He was also clear that their top priority was: education, education, education!

They built their strategy on pressure and support. The former by having explicit targets, and an aggressive, punitive accountability strategy that brought serious consequences (being place on 'special measures' if progress was not made) carried out by the national inspection agency—the Office for Standards in Education (OFSTED). Barber et al. also established an enormous support system for capacity building (to increase the skills and competencies of teachers and administrators to improve teaching and learning, and to work and learn together to increase literacy and numeracy). NLNS (the National Literacy and Numeracy Strategy) was the first comprehensive strategy in the world that used 'capacity building' as one of its central premises. There was a system of local, regional, and national literacy and numeracy leaders, great new curriculum resources, and a network of learning to draw from.

In 1997 a team of us at OISE/UT was invited to bid for a multi-year evaluation of NLNS. We put together a great group; Nancy, my chief researcher, Lorna Earl, one of those great practitioner-academics, and Ken Leithwood, one of the leading researchers in the world on educational leadership (and a contemporary of mine having joined OISE in the same year as me, 1968). For four years we traced the evolution of what was the first attempt in the world at 'whole system change', and filed our final report five years later (Earl et al., 2003). We drew two conclusions. First that the strategy was successful to a point: literacy and numeracy increased from 57% proficiency to 75% in English, and from 54% to 72% in numeracy between 1996 and 2000. Second, we concluded that the results were not sustainable, deep, or likely to last because there was insufficient ownership, and that the negative accountability was taking its toll. The English for example had set annual targets for literacy and numeracy, and then obsessed about their ongoing implementation; this strategy turned out to be the tail that tried to wag a very reluctant dog.

I also found in discussions with teachers in England that I could get away with straight talk (the Shapiro dividend). Union leaders in England were hostile to the NLNS strategy, especially the way it was carried out with punitive accountability. They would have no part of it. I faced a few angry crowds of teachers. In my speeches I would push for professional collaboration as a source of improving teaching. I could see a few backs stiffening as I sensed that they would have no part of it, thinking that teachers are professionals and should have individual autonomy. I persisted with example after example where collaboration led to improvement. I consider one of the greatest compliments that I ever received to be one from a female union leader who came up to me at the end of a heated session and said: "you make some of the things I disagree with, listenable". Impressive empathy on my part, I guess.

I will have more to say about the English strategy, but for now it represented a tidy little message for what was to become my new system work: recalibrate and relegate accountability to the background, and promote capacity building to play a starring role. Later on I had a chance to refine this advice when I became Chief Advisor to the newly elected Premier in Ontario, Dalton McGuinty in October 2003. In any case, the NLNS evaluation was the first great experience that enabled me to learn about the ins and outs of whole system change up close.

The second experience, negative in the sense that it involved an example of 'bad system change', was happening right under my nose in Ontario. There is no federal agency in Canada for education (except for some aspects of First Nations' responsibilities). Each province is entirely autonomous with respect to the public education system. There are three political parties in Ontario: the Conservatives (to the right), the New Democratic Party (NDP, to the left), and the Liberals (straddling the middle shall we say). Around the year 2000 I had started to work with the York Region District School Board (YRDSB), one of currently 72 districts in the province. The Director of Education, Bill Hogarth, asked me to conduct an audit of the system. My advice was: the district is all over the map. You need to focus, focus, focus. And that he did. He and his superintendent of curriculum, Lyn Sharratt, developed a 'literacy and numeracy collaborative' which they pursued for the next nine years with incredibly successful results for a large system, and in so doing became one of the leading boards in the province (subsequent years brought problems to York, but that is a different story and a different book). My FEUT team (Carol Rolheiser, Joanne Quinn from the Learning Consortium, and me) helped lead the capacity building sessions in York during this period in the 2000–2009 decade. Up close, I was seeing and being part of a deliberate system success with over 100,000 students more or less on the heels of our English assessment.

I began to notice what was happening at the Provincial level. The Conservatives under Premier Mike Harris had been elected in 1995 under the banner, Common Sense Revolution. They reduced the number of school boards in the province from 122 to 72. They then proceeded with what could only be called a slash and burn strategy. They reduced the education budget by more than $5bn, and trashed teachers that led to 120,000 teachers walking out in an illegal strike with hundreds of school days lost. The government's harsh messages actually turned public opinion in favor of the teachers (a team of us had conducted a study of the walkout and other strikes and their consequences), and were in constant battle with the education sector—teachers and school boards alike.

By this time Charles Pascal was Executive Director of the Atkinson Foundation (a charitable foundation devoted to issues of social justice). In late 2002 The Foundation decided to fund a team of us, Ken Leithwood, Nancy Watson, and me (essentially the English evaluation team) to conduct a public audit of the Ontario education system under the title: *The schools we need.* In January 2003 we issued a discussion paper that suggested five conditions for system success that must be met: a strong *vision* of the value of a vibrant public school system; *governance* that enabled focus; use of *evidence* relative to how to improve student learning; palpable *support for teachers;* and *adequate and flexible funding.* In other words, pretty much the opposite of what the Conservatives were doing.

After a round of discussions over the next few months we released our final report in April 2003 under the title: *The schools we need: A new blueprint for Ontario* (Leithwood et al., 2003). We blasted the Conservatives for having too many policies; some useful policies that were poorly implemented; some policies that were misguided that were 'at best distracting' and 'at worst harmful', and some glaring policy omissions, such as in early childhood. We called for a total policy overhaul that would be based on the five conditions.

In the meantime (and of course it is no coincidence) the province was gearing up for the next provincial election that was less than six months away (October 2, 2003). The leader of the main opposition—the liberals—was a young wet behind the ears lawyer from Ottawa who had lost the election to Harris in 1999. This time he was more prepared and the conditions were radically different—a public that was increasingly worried about the status of the public school system, and an opposition led by teachers and others who were more organized, more determined, and more knowledgeable about the failure of the present system.

Dalton's Chief of Staff was Gerald Butts (who went on to become Justin Trudeau's Principal Secretary, helping to lead him to being elected as Prime Minister of the country in October 2015). In the spring of 2003 Dalton and team had already decided that education was to be their election platform. They had gone to England earlier in 2003 to learn about Tony Blair's (apparent) success in literacy and numeracy. They met with Michael Barber who gave them chapter and verse, and then said, "actually the person who I go to for advice is Michael Fullan whose office is likely a couple of blocks from yours". On their return I met with Dalton and Gerald and gave them the third edition of my basic book, which was by then called: *The new meaning of educational change* (2001). They called me up a few days later and said "that's our agenda". They invited me to join them, said that I could have any senior policy position I wanted once they were elected.

On October 2, 2003 Dalton McGuinty was elected with a clear majority, and his mandate of 'education, education, education'. I accepted the position of 'Special Advisor to the Premier, and the Minister of Education'. I wanted to be flexible to do other work, and my work as Dean had eventually shown that I could not devote myself fully to an inside job.

Before proceeding to the McGuinty era, and since this book is about education change ideas, this would be a good time to ask 'where do my ideas come from'? Here is another update on the idea front.

Change Ideas 2003

If I had to express, as a seminal idea, the response to the question of where my ideas come from it would be this:

> *Seminal Idea #6: My ideas come from a mixture of doing change, reading, and writing.*

Note that research per se is not on the list. I don't conduct much research in the traditional sense. Andy Hargreaves, for example, immerses himself and his team in large-scale change research, and takes more than a year to mine and shape what he has found (then he writes quickly and deeply). I 'do change': help it out, lead it, consult on it, do reviews and evaluations. And I write quickly. Later I will add training and workshops to the doing category to come up with seminal idea #7. As I am doing change I read widely. I am always on the hunt for new ideas and know them when I see them—like Seymour Sarason's 'culture of the school'. Third, I write my way to clarity and insight. These three actions and interactions—do, read, write—create an amalgam from which come the change ideas and revelations.

Each edition of 'the meaning' (three by 2001) kept me on the boil. My books have moved from theory-driven to practice driven. *Change forces* (1993) and *Change forces: The sequel* (1999) are theory based, but in the domain of moral purpose, and making sense of complexity. I read a lot of the business book literature (advice: 90% of it is superficial, confusing, and contradictory). Periodically I write a book intended for both education and business audiences. My first one was *Leading in a culture of change* (2001) in which I presented a five-fold model: moral purpose, understanding change, relationship building, knowledge creation and sharing, and coherence making. Then *The moral imperative of school leadership* (2003), and the third in the change forces trilogy, *Change forces with a vengeance* (2003) where I brought together: moral purpose writ large, new lessons for complex change, tri-level reform (local schools, districts, the state), and leadership and sustainability. The doing and the writing are a mutual feed. I will give more updates about change ideas as we go, including in the postscript, where I reflect on how the subconscious and the surreal might interact to produce surprising results.

In the rest of this chapter I will take up the Dalton Days (2003–2012) that first got me involved in helping to lead system change. In Chapter 6 I will turn to the Global Days (2013–2017) that include being advisor to Premier Kathleen Wynne who succeeded Dalton (same political party), but also encompass the increasingly present global quest to have the best education system in the world

The Dalton Days: 2003–2012

Premier McGuinty was elected October 2, 2003, and a week later Michael Barber who happened to be in Toronto and I met with the

Premier and his Minister of Education, Gerard Kennedy. By then I had known what we should do initially. Literacy, numeracy, and high school graduation had been flat lined for four years as measured by the provincial agency, the Educational Quality and Accountability Office (EQAO); the Ministry of Education did not have the capacity to lead the change; conflict with teachers had been festering for six years and needed to be addressed. We would need to initiate it from the top, but then develop it jointly with the sector—the 72 districts, 4900 schools, and the teachers. Organizationally it meant that we would have to set up a focused fast track entity (in this case the Literacy Numeracy Secretariat; LNS) within the larger and 'slower' Ministry of Education to get things done.

My proposal was on one page:

First, make literacy, numeracy, and high school graduation priorities with named targets (more about targets shortly). Focus on reducing the gap between higher and lower performing groups and schools. (Later we added 'increase the confidence of the public in the public school system'). At the same time, establish a new unit within the Ministry of Education, called The Literacy Numeracy Secretariat (LNS) and staff it with a mixture of respected change leaders and experts in the sector, and existing Ministry personnel.

Second, focus on capacity building linked to results working with the sector to jointly develop and monitor solutions. We added: Develop a Peace and Stability Strategy vis-à-vis the Teacher Unions.

We did not go for a task force or any other big vision strategy. The main problems needed attention; we thought we knew how to jump into the fray and get immediate progress. It was characteristic of my relationship with Premier McGuinty and his staff that we came to decisions rather quickly (in relation to typical government timelines). I can only highlight the key actions and developments in this book (for a more detailed account of the Ontario Story see Fullan & Rincón-Gallardo, 2016). In the next few pages I will review the main issues and accomplishments in the crucial first three years.

First, from England we had identified two positive and two negative lessons. On the negative side were, don't obsess with targets, and don't engage in punitive accountability. On the positive side of the ledger: make sure you *focus* on a small number of priorities; and invest in *capacity building* (strategies to improve instruction, and to develop people's capacity to collaborate and learn from each other).

On the question of targets we did know the base line in Ontario: around 54% high proficiency in literacy and math, and 68% graduation rates. We set targets of 75% for literacy and math and 85% for graduation from our 900 high schools. We were careful to say that the targets were aspirational and as long as we were making steady progress things would be fine. (If you are curious about the eventual outcomes by 2017, 12 years or so later, we are close to 75% literacy, 85% high school graduation, but got stuck at 60% math. Except for math and continuing to work on reducing the gap in several subcategories most people consider the outcomes to be a success.)

Second, we established LNS during 2004, appointing one of the leading directors in the province, Avis Glaze, an outstanding educator, and person. Avis then staffed LNS with over 100 educators, many of them seconded from districts working on three-year rotating terms, and organized into teams that worked with clusters of ten or 11 districts each. A key lesson here is that governments need a fast track approach to launching new initiatives. Avis is one of Ontario's global education leaders, and has now become a worldwide sought after advisor and speaker.

Third, Premier McGuinty was active in implementation. He chaired what amounted to a 'Guiding Coalition', which consisted of the Minister of Education, the deputy minister, head of LNS, other senior officials, and me. We met every six weeks for three years, reviewing progress, making corrections, developing better strategies, and celebrating success. Interestingly, the public at large might be surprised at the engaged, active and at times aggressive role that Dalton played in those meetings, given his public persona as a smart but somewhat introverted nice guy. In these meetings he was demanding: "sorry that doesn't seem to be good enough"; "this plan does not have enough detail"; "bring me a plan at the next meeting that has evidence of progress", and so on.

Fourth, the Minister of Education, Gerard Kennedy, tackled the 'peace and stability' agenda. He and his Chief of Staff, Katie Telford (who is now Prime Minister Justin Trudeau's Chief of Staff working again with Gerald Butts), accomplished something that I thought was impossible. There were five different teacher unions: elementary public, secondary public, elementary and secondary Catholic (also public), francophone, and an umbrella organization called the Ontario Teachers' Federation. And there were many more unions for support staff and civil servants. Moreover collective bargaining was local (72 districts, times many more subunits including unions related to administrative staffing unions). Somehow Gerard and Katie, through strong and soft arming, and many all-nighters got everyone to agree to an overall financial framework, which in one sense was not even legal (it wasn't illegal, but wasn't required legally). That framework which took local 'financial' bargaining off the local table into a province-wide arena has served us to the present. In the four years prior to 2003 there were hundreds of teacher days lost to strikes; in the four years after 2003 the number was zero.

Fifth, we handled the accountability dilemma quite well. Punitive accountability was the bane of the English failure, but resorting to 'no accountability' was clearly not an acceptable alternative. We did two things. We made it clear that there would be no direct action taken against schools or districts on EQAO results. Second, we treated the results as indicators of progress or not with the emphasis on capacity building. We actually trained ourselves to be non-judgmental, which is to say that when you see low performance your reaction needs to be, what capacity building is needed here. We revamped the Ontario Focused Intervention Program (OFIP)—intended to turn around low performing schools—so that it was seen as a positive opportunity rather than a stigma. Through this we reduced the number of low performing elementary schools from over 800 to fewer than 60. In many ways addressing accountability is as much in the *attitude* as it is in the actual strategy. If you get it right you get greater internal accountability, which consists of people taking responsibility in a transparent way for their own individual and collective progress.

When I was about a year and a half into the job as advisor I had a heart attack in the summer of 2004. I was at the cottage, three hours from Toronto and Wendy drove me to the hospital in the middle of the night (stupid on our part not to get an ambulance). I didn't get treated for five hours (the drive plus waiting in the emergency room). I don't remember being the least bit panicky. Somehow I was suddenly transferred from one hospital to the top cardiac one in Toronto, given a stent, and put under the care of arguably the top research cardiologist in Toronto, Dr. John Floras. I don't know how this happened. Maybe it was some kind of hidden Harry Walker who intervened. Once more surreal things were happening. Dr. Floras said it was his job to keep me alive a decade at a time (I am now in year 14, and have just asked him to promise me another decade). What a bedside manner; he didn't want me to worry in the short run. He got to know that I travelled all the time (basically non-stop from September to June) and we made appointments around my schedule. The only advice he gave me was don't sleep with my head fully down on the long-haul flights which were plenty. My general practitioner, Dr McKellar, has done his share of keeping me as healthy as possible.

I am hoping that my dominant genes come from my mother's side of the family. She died in her 90s; my euchre playing aunts lived to 90; my grandfather and his mother lived late into their 90s. On my father's side, not so good. His father, Thomas (known as Will), died in 1945 at age 69 from a heart attack driving down Pape Street in eastern Toronto. I was five years old about to receive my own invasion of father and brothers. My father died in 1992 at age 76 (a year younger than I am as I write these words) after a heart attack and a couple of strokes, but he wasn't leading a meaningful life most of his last ten years. And he didn't have Dr. Floras and modern medicine. Anyway, I was back to my regular schedule in 2004 within a few months. My mother was to die in her 90s in 2010. I always felt that she sacrificed her considerable talents for her seven boys. She always expressed her pride of my accomplishments all through her last 20 years. I am the one who should be proud of her.

Relative to the student learning agenda, after a flat line start for one year (which we consider normal), the numbers started moving up and continued to do so except for math. McGuinty was re-elected in 2007 largely on his track record in education. The conservative opposition leader unadvisedly promoted a policy to extend funding to faith-based schools, which was roundly rejected by the public who were committed to public education. After the election we strengthened our resolve on the core agenda that included closing the gap between subgroups. We saw major gains in reducing the gaps for immigrants (Ontario has a steady influx of students who don't speak English), for special education students, and to a certain extent for boys compared to girls. Public opinion also favored what was happening in the education sector.

We then turned to early learning—a topic which advocates and the evidence had shown for years was critical for reducing the gap and getting off to stronger starts for the 0–5 age group. By that time the province had a considerable budget deficit ($18bn). Leading early learning advocates—Margaret McCain and Fraser Mustard, and Charles Pascal at Atkinson—had already made the case that early learning was a high need–high payoff area. The group was frustrated at not being able to get action from the Premier so they requested that Chuck ask me to talk to Dalton (I did not know the early learning research in detail). Chuck took me out to breakfast and made two points: 28% of children in Ontario are seriously vulnerable when they reach grade 1, and most don't catch up; and that we are now demonstrating the kind of pedagogy and curriculum that will make a difference. I said, "I got it". Incidentally, I love what we call 'simplexity': a few key understandable points that are complex but powerful when implemented. I did not in fact run to see the Premier. We did discuss early learning briefly, noted that we should consider action at some point, but I waited for him to raise the matter.

Sure enough the Premier called me for a meeting shortly after being re-elected in 2007 to talk about early learning. I knew it would be a short meeting because of our earlier discussion. We had said we should move to do something in this area, and that whatever we did should be all in, not piecemeal. So it was decided to appoint a one-person commission as Special Advisor to the Premier who would take a year of investigation, research, and regional hearings in order to advise on *how, not whether* to implement early learning. The Premier invited Charles Pascal to take on the role. After a year of research, demonstration projects, and the input of over 20,000 individuals and groups, Charles submitted his report in June 2009, *With our best future in mind: Implementing early learning in Ontario* (Pascal, 2009).

It took us one meeting to decide what to do. We would follow Pascal's report and establish Early Learning for all 4- and 5-year-olds in the province (250,000 children in total) and phase it in over a three-year period: Septembers, 2010, 2011, 2012. Assistant Deputy Jim Grieve was appointed to head the implementation team, and we problem solved as we went. It was actually quite complicated: staffing (we decided to have a certified teacher and early learning certified person in each class); space (where to find accommodation with the goal that early learning and elementary schools should be integrated under one principal); curriculum (what is a play based curriculum anyway); and assessment (what are the markers of progress). A number of people were key to making the implementation of early learning a success: Charles worked with Jim Grieve, and with Dalton's key policy advisors John Broadhead and Pierina DeCarolis to ensure that decisions along the way were evidence based. Incidentally, I always worked closely with the chief policy advisors of the politicians. They are key members of the political team, have great detail, and by definition daily access to the Premier and the Minister.

The early learning agenda had been in the wings for years, but once it was decided we acted quickly: a solid blueprint, a process that was transparent, a tabled report in June of 2009, and phase one implementation that started in 2010. When was a commission's results acted on so quickly?

As far as McGuinty is concerned it took considerable courage and what he often called his moral compass to plunk down a further $2bn on top of an $18bn deficit, believing that the evidence would prove him right (which incidentally it did including a 2017 external evaluation that shows conclusively that 4- and 5-year-olds who receive good early learning do considerably better by the time they arrive in grade 1; Pelletier, 2017). One of the reasons I so enjoyed working with McGuinty is that he was evidence based, at least when it came to education. He read detailed briefs and articles I would send him, and he followed up with great questions. When he acted he drew upon these and other materials.

The liberal party and McGuinty struggled as they headed for the third-term election in the fall of 2011. The worldwide recession in 2008 undercut revenues; and there was the decision to cancel the development of two electrical gas plants that were under construction that cost the taxpayers $1bn, and was widely seen as a blatant move to get votes in the affected constituencies. The election occurred and the liberals were re-elected but had one seat short of a majority.

The next year was quite complicated. Essentially, McGuinty and the liberals were obsessed with picking up one seat through a by-election in order to re-claim their majority. They made some questionable moves that included getting tough on teachers with respect to the next round of collective bargaining. A new piece of legislation—Bill 115—was eventually passed (September 2012) limiting some of the rights of unions with respect to strikes and other matters. After eight years of 'peace and stability' the lid was blown off the relationships with teachers. Why? For whatever reason, the Premier was listening to a few political hardliners, who knew little about the context of our success in education. I won't talk about my own role in this (other than to say that I and some others told the Premier that the hard line tactics were going to backfire). The end result was that McGuinty's popularity plummeted, and an impasse with teachers ensued. McGuinty prorogued the government (essentially shutting it down) in order to take stock, and suddenly resigned from his position as Premier in the fall of 2012. Dalton McGuinty, a Premier who loved public education and did something about it, had temporarily lost his way. Despite this serious misstep, McGuinty's legacy is a public education system that to this day is one of the leaders in the world.

Before continuing we need to take a detour to consider other things that were happening in the world of whole system change that turned out to be precursors to the 2013–2017 period.

Meanwhile in the Rest of the World: 2003–2011

As fascinating as the McGuinty years were we need to get back to the main purpose of this book, which is to locate the main change ideas for system reform in terms of the particular moment in history in which they were occurring. I will require Andy Hargreaves for this role.

Andy Hargreaves and Me

As Andy and I finished the *What's worth fighting for* trilogy in 1998 he proceeded quite appropriately to develop his career. As Assistant Director Academic I was happy to support him as he established a new 'Center for Education Change' and a new journal, the *Journal of*

Educational Change. As a faculty member he was a senior leader's dream: bringing on lots of research grants, and being productive and innovative on all fronts. We also sat down one day at lunch (by that time I was Dean of FEUT) and we agreed that it was time for him to head for a new setting and challenge. Before long he was offered and took up the Brennan Chair in Education at Boston College in 2002. I supported him fully in this move.

Andy then began to carve deeply into his own career (he can write his own auto-bio so I am just going to cover the issues that relate to my change ideas and evolution). As I mentioned earlier, I always felt from the beginning that I nudged him into becoming more applied, and he steered me deeper. He didn't need much nudging because he has become quite good at, innovative about, and morally committed to solutions.

Predictably, as Andy got better at analysis and solutions we clashed. He had a real anathema to the Blair–Barber LNS strategy, which he saw as narrow, top-down and ultimately undermining the teaching profession and the quality of education for students. There might have been some English working class rebellion on Andy's end as part of the equation. It was a moral and analytic issue for him. As he began to work more widely he found a strong affinity with Alberta, a highly successful province that built its success through strong partnership with the Alberta Teachers Association and the CASS, the College of Alberta School Superintendents. He felt that, unfairly, Ontario was being profiled as successful when it was Alberta that in his assessment was better (incidentally, I agree with Andy about the question of 'fairness'. Ontario was much more plugged into the international comparison crowd, and consequently got more publicity than Alberta). I knew Alberta was good because I was also working with them through CASS—the superintendents' association.

Around 2006, and from a distance, Andy saw the Ontario strategy as a replica of the English strategy. We had literacy and numeracy as priorities, an implementation secretariat, I had evaluated England's NLNS, and Michael Barber was a friend of Ontario, and so on. Andy began to criticize the Ontario strategy (we travelled in the same circles, and were frequently on the same podium together). I began to resent it because I knew that it was wrong to equate the Ontario and English strategy, that our teachers were more respected and involved, and that Andy did not have any first-hand knowledge as he had been away since we began the strategy in 2004. We had some pretty heated disagreements late at night on email because we were both quick and set in our conclusions.

So we fought in small doses around the world as we ended up on the same panels and platforms. On one occasion, around 2010, we were on the stage in Sydney (I think at the aquarium; all those sharks!) in front of a large national audience from the Australian Council of Education Leaders. Andy is a great orator and he was taking some veiled and distorted shots at countries that had tests (read Ontario, I thought). He was playing to the sentiment of those whom he knew were against government intervention. I made my counter points—assessment can be useful if you avoid punitive accountability, and do not obsess on results. After the session was over I had a moment with him where I said, "I hate when you play to the crowd". In less than a heartbeat he replied with indignation, "I never play to the crowd for political reasons, only for pedagogical reasons". What! For me this was a distinction without a difference.

The sparring reached a high point (more accurately a low point) at the International Congress of School Principals bi-annual meeting that was held in Toronto in 2011. We were a two-man panel. We traded a few barbs, and out of the blue Andy broke into full-throated song, "You've lost that loving feeling". I thought it must have been premeditated because he had changed some of the words. Picture Andy singing directly to me on a big stage. You wanted surreal!

Andy and I had been referred to now and then as the Righteous Brothers (or was it Self-Righteous as each of us seemed to think of the other?). I was a bit stymied and I replied with an (unattributed) Nietzche quote: "the trouble with you Andy is that you muddy the waters to make them appear deep". He immediately shot back, "I do that so that you can walk on them". The audience—principals from all over the world—were stunned, and/or bemused. Later people variously said: what was Andy doing; that was bizarre and so on. Some said it was great theatre: two gladiators going after each other. It was one time when my lack of emotion served me well. I don't think either Andy or I felt odd about the exchange, but it was clearly becoming weird.

If the truth were to be told, Andy and I were never very far apart on the main substantive issues. There was some odd rivalry going on that would take the psychiatrist's couch to unravel, which I am not going to attempt to do. As it turns out two breakthroughs were on the horizon. The minor (but still crucial) one came when Andy and his team conducted a study of ten school districts in Ontario resulting in a publication *Leading for all* (Hargreaves & Braun, 2012). Andy had finally taken a close look at Ontario, and broadly he liked what he saw. The ten lessons that Hargreaves and Braun derived were consistent with what we thought we were doing (encouraging local leadership, promoting collective responsibility, evidence informed decision making, linking technology and pedagogy in ways that increased precision and impact on learning). Andy and his team had additional insights and critiques about the Ontario strategy, but they were more grounded and targeted. From then on Andy showed a growing respect for Ontario, and his criticisms became fewer and more accurate.

Our differences are minor, around the edges, and complementary. He thought that my agenda was too narrow (literacy, numeracy, graduation) and that I wanted to control the change process too much. I thought his agenda was too broad, and that he left too much to chance. We both moved to appreciate and learn from each other. The major vehicle, which amounted to a spiritual conversion, was writing a new book together. Carole Saltz, the great chief editor from Teachers College Press (the very publisher (but different editor) that gave me my first breakthrough with *The meaning of educational change* book) was after us to do a sequel to our *What's worth fighting for* work which we had published with Teachers College Press. Months and a couple of years went by and we were not getting anywhere—not even close to starting. Finally one day Andy said, "our hearts and minds are not into a revised edition, let's write a brand new book on the teaching profession".

Andy had written good analytic books on teachers but this time we wanted to combine our talents that linked deep concepts, and fundamental applied solutions. We were ready, both individually and together, for this book in 2011 in a way that would have been impossible even a year previously. Once we got started you couldn't have stopped us with a locomotive. We had rejected book titles like 'Teach like a pro'. Along the way in rapid order the innovative ideas started to come. Most of the initial insights were Andy's: the concepts of business and professional capital, adding decisional capital at the last moment, and so on.

I recognized a good idea as soon as I glimpsed it. If you are immersed in learning and change the way I was by 2011 you get to the point where you recognize potential great ideas in their preformed state. It is actually surreal. You recognize things before other people do. You literally see things that other people can't see. And once you surface them people say, I wish I had thought of that, I knew that, and so on. I mentioned before that my goal (forte?) in writing is to present something that people in a given situation will read and say, it was as if he were in my shoes. It is more than that. People say to me, you told me something about myself that I knew, but was not conscious of until you articulated it. Incidentally, this is what Michael Polyani was getting at when he observed that in tacit knowledge "we know more than we can tell" (this is the theme of the two books I mentioned in Chapter 1: *Nuance*, and *The devil is in the details* which, by the way, are not written yet).

Andy and I wrote feverishly, night after night. The only differences we had led to deeper insights. The final product, *Professional capital: Transforming teaching in every school* (Hargreaves & Fullan, 2012), is the most original, deepest book I have ever been associated with. I don't mention in this professional autobiography the various awards I have received over the years, except if they are associated with a big change idea. *Professional capital* merits this recognition. In 2015, it won the coveted Grawemeyer Prize, which is awarded annually and "recognizes the power a single creative idea can have on the world". Andy and I had arrived—together! The idea was professional capital as a foundational concept for understanding and developing the teaching profession—a resource that once started keeps on giving. There was also a seminal idea in Andy's and my reunion at a much deeper level than ever before.

Seminal Idea #7: When you are in conflict with someone who has good ideas, and good values, build don't burn bridges.

I need to go out of sequence here and jump to 2016. In that year Andy and I had an opportunity to build on *Professional capital*. The large staff development organization Learning Forward (LF) was scheduled to hold its annual 2016 conference in Vancouver; a year in advance they commissioned Carol Campbell to lead a research team to assess the state of professional learning in Canada. Carol and her team wrote a magnificent comprehensive study finding such subtleties as Canadian teachers did not find workshops as problematic as their US peers because they always felt they had a choice about whether to use the ideas, whereas US teachers seemed to fear (realistically I would say) ideas being imposed. Stephanie Hirsch, the President of LF, asked Andy and me to write a call to action based on the Campbell report. We had a ridiculously short hard timeline because we had to finish and present the report in Vancouver in early December 2016 with less than a month to complete our work. This writing was like magic. We ripped into the writing, sharing drafts and sections and cross critiquing on the fly. It was early November 2016 and several odd or unusual things happened. First, Andy and I were both scheduled to give keynotes in Bogota, Colombia. We had been invited by Vicky Colbert to help celebrate the 30th anniversary of her highly successful rural education Escuela Nueva program. Initially I was especially interested to go because I had followed the peace negotiations between the government and the rebel group FARC who had been engaged in a long-standing bloody conflict that had killed 220,000 people over a 55-year period. The two parties—the government and the rebels—had reached a seeming agreement that was being put to a referendum in October—a month before we were scheduled to go. The agreement failed to win a majority by a slight margin (some people were unhappy that FARC members would be granted amnesty). I hesitated to go expecting that new conflict would erupt. Andy decided to attend and I decided that I should go as well. As it turned out a month or so later Colombia forged ahead with the peace agreement and is now implementing it. If you want to think in terms of moral purpose Latin America has great promise— 50 million people in Colombia alone. Education will be its next route to freedom and prosperity. Incidentally, 13 months later in December 2017, Vicky was awarded the inaugural Yidan Prize in Education Development garnering $3.9 million to support the further development and expansion of Escuela Nueva in Colombia and worldwide.

Second, Andy and I were still faced with the hard deadline for the Learning Forward report so we grabbed every moment we could to work on it within the Bogota conference, which was taking place in early November. One day we found a quiet corner to huddle together and resolve some issues only to be discovered by a senior sociologist from Chile who was at the same conference. We did not know him but he overheard some of our conversation and inserted himself into the discussion citing this and that research. It was actually comical as we politely responded while trying to slip in some agreements on points that we were working on.

Third, that evening, November 7, 2016 the Canadian poet, singer, and songwriter Leonard Cohen died. Andy had been a long time fan, but my connection was only in the last two years. No one can listen to 'Everybody knows' (that the dice are loaded), or 'Hallelujah' and not feel your emotions disturbed. But it was his most recent and final album released October 21, less than three weeks before his death, that was the ultimate. Andy and I had marvelled at it when it first appeared: "You want it darker; We kill the flame". Cohen had not predicted his death as much as projected himself into the afterlife. He literally seems to have willed his own denouement! That evening Andy and I traded Cohen lyrics by email from our own rooms while individually listening to Cohen songs (had we been two women we might have gotten together in one of our rooms, but we were nonetheless communal in our quiet individual retreats). I felt a profound, unfathomable sense of emotions that I could not characterize. The best I can come up with is I felt human—vulnerable but very much alive.

Fourth, the next night, November 8 and into the 9th Donald Trump got elected President of the US. The world was speechless. Overall those few days in early November evoked an unusual and intense sense of being alive in the midst of human turmoil and promise.

We still had our Learning Forward report to finish and a few days later we were at Quest, York Region's annual conference, and met on Andy's arrival at 11pm to sort out some ideas. The final writing continued from a distance with rapid back and forth via email. It is no exaggeration to say that the writing was surreal. It took no time to resolve matters, and generate brand new ideas and insights. I had had 'flow-like' experiences a few times before when writing solo, but never in paired writing. Andy said the same. Maybe the Righteous Brothers had become the Stones! Mick and Keith get along these days, don't they?

Andy and I produced a call for action for LF under the title *Bringing the profession back in*, and for fun flipped a coin to determine the order of authorship, and the report became Fullan & Hargreaves (2016) with the agreement that we would reverse the order in the next publication.

We also had a breakthrough idea in that report that finally settled the question of whether autonomy or collaboration should dominate. The answer of course is *both* are required and must feed on each other. We had solidified the definition of collaborative professionalism. Andy went on in 2017 to conduct a strong global study of collaborative professionalism.

> *Seminal Idea #8: Autonomy is not isolation. You need collaboration to be effective autonomously, and vice versa. Collaborative professionalism honors both the individual and the collective.*

Of course idea #8 is an inevitable derivative of our Grawemeyer Prize idea; namely, the future of education depends a great deal on the *professional capital of teachers (human, social, and decisional).*

What Else in 2003–2012?

We have seen the productive Dalton Days, and the Andy rapprochement. Things were heating up on other fronts. I had written an article for the *Journal of Educational Change* in 2000 titled 'The return of large-scale reform' (Fullan, 2000). I was reading the tea leaves, and projecting my own interests when I identified eight factors or insights:

1 Upgrade system context (revamping policies, incentives, standards, etc. for the teaching profession).
2 Become pre-occupied with coherence making in the service of instructional improvement and student learning.
3 Establish plenty of crossover structures.
4 Downward investment/upward identity.
5 Invest in quality materials.
6 Integrate pressure and support (set targets, build capacity).
7 Get out of implementing someone else's reform agenda.
8 Work with systems.

Of course this was still 'theory'; I hadn't done it yet. I took these ideas into the Dalton Days and learned a great deal more through action on the ground in the ten years 2003–2012. We continued to build great teams. Gerald Butts and Katie Telford left shortly after the 2007 election and were replaced by Jamison Steeve and Pierina Decarolis in the Premier's office who were fabulous to work with for the subsequent five years. We continued to add capacity within the government. In 2005 we hired Carol Campbell, a very young student of policy making from Great Britain (and who is Scottish), and placed her in LNS where she became head of research (practical research 'don't you know') for all of the Ministry of Education. Within a decade Carol was to become a young, global superstar in the field of policy studies. Avis Glaze had built LNS into a powerful entity and partner to the field with respect to the basic agenda. When it came time to replace Avis we appointed Mary Jean Gallagher in 2008. Like Avis, Mary Jean was a leading Director of Education (in this case from the Windsor area), and had already proven that system improvement was possible under very difficult circumstances. Mary Jean further strengthened LNS (and in 2016 came to work with me on broader system change in the world—we will co-author *The devil is in the details* book).

I continued to write books that were fed by my work in Ontario, and increasingly around the world. *The moral imperative of school leadership* came in 2003 with what was to become one of my strongest new publishers, Corwin Press (Fullan, 2003b). Then *Leadership and sustainability: System thinkers in action* (Fullan, 2005), *Turnaround leadership* (Fullan, 2006), *Breakthrough* in 2006 with two of the greatest practitioners I know—husband and wife team, Peter Hill (policy maker) and Carmel Crévola (trainer extraordinaire)—who really should publish more, but at least I got to learn from them, and we made it available to the world (Fullan et al., 2006). The fourth edition of *The new meaning of educational change* came in 2007 (Fullan, 2007); *The six secrets of change*, a business book in 2008 (Fullan, 2008). Another book was a foray into higher education, *Turnaround leadership for higher education* (Fullan & Scott, 2009), with a former doctoral student at OISE, Geoff Scott, who was an expert in changing cultures in universities. Geoff was famous for his response to a question in his dissertation defense when one of the unimaginative examiners asked him the routine question, "if you had it to do over again what would you have done differently in your thesis?" Not being good at controlling his

Aussie humor Geoff blurted out "I would have used my brain"! He knew he had already proven himself during his defense.

Still another book was *All systems go* in 2010 with chapters like: collective capacity building, the idea of whole system reform, and politicians and professionals unite (Fullan, 2010a); *Motion leadership: The skinny on becoming change savvy* in 2010, arising from our workshops (more about the critical role of workshops in my development in a moment) (Fullan, 2010b); *The moral imperative realized* (pushing more into impact) in 2011 (Fullan, 2011c); another business book, *Change leader* came the same year (Fullan, 2011a). Also came two books with Lyn Sharratt, the superintendent of curriculum with whom I had worked in the York Region: *Realization: The change imperative for deepening district-wide reform* (Sharratt & Fullan, 2009), and *Putting FACES on the data* (Sharratt & Fullan, 2012). Lyn has gone on to become an outstanding consultant and workshop leader working in many places that I do, such as Australia. In this same period Andy and I published our treasured coming out treatise, *Professional capital* (2012). I wrote other books with some of the leading practitioners of the day (such as Rick Dufour, Mr. 'Professional Learning Community' himself), and a slew of articles over the years, but I won't list them here other than to say, I wanted to have a continuous presence in the field of policy and practice.

Early in this period I had started to travel with the international crowd. I had got to know many of them through our LNS evaluation. Michael Barber of course; the Australian Tony McKay (who is the world's greatest facilitator) whom I refer to as 'ubiquitous but ephemeral' as he seems to be everywhere; David Hopkins, the Welshman who tackles mountains and system change with equal aplomb; Steve Munby, the first head of the National College of School Leadership in England, and a brilliant leader in his own right; and Andreas Schleicher, the head of the OECD education division, Dr. Pisa himself, and many more. In 2004, we (Dalton et al.) had set as one of our goals, 'international presence in the area of system change where we would contribute to and learn from other countries in the world'. In Chapter 6 we will meet some other international stars who will broaden our perspective in 2013 and the following period.

The Power of Training/Workshops Vehicles for Learning

We might as well start with the seminal idea.

Seminal Idea #9: Eighty percent of your best ideas come from your leading customers.

These days when I am seeking an insight on a given issue my first port of call is not research or other professors, but rather it is 'leading practitioners'—a shift that began with my new style of writing in 1987 with *What's worth fighting for*, increased with my leadership roles from 1988 onward, really intensified with workshops around the world starting shortly after 2000, and was captured in my books *Motion leadership* (2010b), and *Motion leadership in action* (2013b) that featured by name several practitioner leaders like Trish Okoruwa from Hackney, London, Miguel Brechner, Uruguay, Jim Watterston, Australia, and John Malloy from Ontario who is currently the Director of the mega Toronto District School Board.

When it came to workshops (teaching really), I was a pretty hopeless academic when I arrived at FEUT to be Dean in 1988. During the next decade I was exposed to cooperative learning and other techniques of engagement through some of the young faculty we hired, and the workshops we carried out through the Learning Consortium. But my handlers would not yet let me get in front of a group by myself.

In 2000 I decided to link 'engaged learning and change' into an open-to-the-world workshop called *Breaking Barriers*. Our best young trainer, Assistant Professor Carol Rolheiser, was my mentor and co-presenter. We offered the workshop in 2000 and 2001 in Toronto and it was a huge success. One of the attendees in both years was Alan Boyle, based in London, former curriculum director in a Local Authority, and now interested in training. What followed was a phenomenal decade where Alan organized annual tours in the United Kingdom and Ireland every May, where we would go town to town conducting daily workshops 9am–4pm over a three-week period, on leadership for change. He became my agent and co-worker in the UK and Ireland. Alan organized the tours, my chief assistant and another great team member Claudia Cuttress produced the graphics and provided technical support and helped run the workshops. A couple of years later we added Australia and New Zealand as annual tour destinations, and for the subsequent decade conducted another set of daily workshops every October–November down under. Over the decade we carried out over 300 workshops. Later on Alan and I wrote a book, *Big-city reform*, where we compared the cities of New York, Toronto, and Hackney (a London borough) over a ten-year period (Fullan & Boyle, 2014).

The workshops fed and were fed by my books. Twice a year we had to figure how to convey the latest ideas, and to learn from the workshops. So many of my best ideas, my ability to be in practitioners' shoes, and my capacity to discover from those doing the work 'more than they could tell' (but I could see) came from this decade of engagement. To take one example, Jim Watterston (a great leader in his own right), the Director General of the Australian Capital Territory (ACT), invited us to help him transform a somewhat stagnant system of some 80 schools. In the first year we were in Canberra secondary school where they had trained three teachers as peer coaches using a quality teaching framework. The idea was that they would observe and give feedback to teachers. When we were in the school, at the beginning most teachers went out of their way to tell us that they were not going to participate ('we don't want anyone, especially our peers to watch us teach and tell us how to teach better'). The administration did a number of things to reassure the teachers: participation is voluntary; we want a few of you to try it; when you try it you don't have to accept feedback, just listen to it, etc. When we came back three years later 100% of the teachers were engaged in the peer coaching. There was more excitement about teaching, more sharing, and students noticed an improvement. At the end of the day I sat down with the deputy and said: "This is impressive. Three years ago you had massive resistance, and now mostly with the same people there is 100% involvement and excitement". Then I asked him the killer change question: Is participation in the peer coaching voluntary or mandatory? Without a split second of delay he replied: "it is voluntary but inevitable!" This led to the following new insight:

Seminal Idea #10: Successful change processes are a function of shaping and reshaping good ideas as they build capacity and ownership.

The point is that workshops, well done, represent an opportunity for the *presenter to learn* thereby getting fresh insights that could not be discovered in any other way. The biggest discovery came straight out of the field. On October 2010 we had just finished one of our annual workshops hosted by Tony MacKay and his Centre for Strategic Evaluation (CSE) in Melbourne. We were sipping a nice bottle of Australian Shiraz, and examining evaluations from the day, when Tony and his chief executive Barbara Waterston, and Claudia who worked with me, observed that the ideas were really hitting home. They then suggested that I write a paper for their CSE's policy series. It took us about five minutes to come up with the title: *Choosing the wrong drivers for whole system reform.* That paper became the breakthrough idea for the California reform that I take up in the next chapter. A driver is a policy, and a wrong driver is a policy that does not work. The four wrong drivers were: punitive accountability, individualistic solutions, technology, and ad hoc policy. Their 'right' counterparts were: capacity building, collaboration, pedagogy, systemness (coordinated policies that people at all levels identify with).

My book, *Motion leadership: The skinny on becoming change savvy* (2010), with its eight guidelines for action (relationships first, beware of fat plans, communication during implementation is more important than communication prior to implementation, and so on) came on the heels of a series of workshops.

Along the way, by 2012, the world in Ontario and elsewhere was changing. Dalton had resigned, Ontario had to re-sort itself, and the world was abuzz about what should be next for system reform in education. We had refined the strategies for literacy, and high school graduation, and had built a strong teaching profession in Ontario, but things were shifting in the world. People began asking for a wider and deeper agenda. Societies were becoming more unequal, technology was taking off, students were unsettled with traditional schooling, well-being of students was being questioned. It wouldn't take much for these disturbances to catapult into the spotlight. I had a sense that business as usual would soon be off the table. Something big was about to happen.

6
THE SYSTEM YEARS PART TWO: 2013–2017

I am beginning to know the meaning of the phrase 'life is a journey not a blueprint'. But there are emerging patterns that seem downright evolutionary. I'll return to this matter in the Postscript, but before that let's finish the journey. I will do this in four ways that occurred in parallel in these last five years. First, what is evolving in Ontario in the post Dalton years? Second, what about the surprising (or was it inevitable) uptake of the right drivers on the part of California? Third, my continued love affair with practitioners. Fourth, how did I get involved in the next pedagogical revolution that we call *Deep Learning*? In the Postscript I will return to the global scene with some final comments.

Premier Kathleen Wynne

Just as he was departing Dalton asked me to write a position paper on what we had accomplished, and what might be the next phase. The result was a 14-page paper in 2013 called, *Great to excellent: Launching the next stage of Ontario's education agenda* (Fullan, 2013a). It was really advice to no one as there was nobody at the helm: the government was prorogued (temporarily shut down). In *Great to excellent* I noted the Ontario success and external evaluations that confirmed it, and made two recommendations. One was to 'sustain and build on the improvements we had', and the second was to engage in focused innovation related to the 6Cs of higher order skills (character, citizenship, collaboration, communication, creativity, and critical thinking). As far as I know I was the first one to connect character, and citizenship to the other four well known Cs that were called the 21st century skills. I am not even sure where my idea came from, but see the section later on Deep Learning. I knew that the 21st century skills had been going nowhere and I wanted to come up with something that was exciting, comprehensive, mutually exclusive, and concise; thus, the 6Cs.

In January 2013 the liberal party elected Kathleen Wynne to replace McGuinty. Wynne had held several ministerial offices including Minister of Education 2006–2010. The new Premier took office in February 2013, and eventually went to the polls and won a majority on June 12, 2014. Much of the early part of her premiership involved patching up and re-establishing relationships with the teacher unions that had deteriorated badly in the last days of McGuinty's reign. In late 2013 the Wynne government engaged in a province wide consultation about a 'renewed vision' for Ontario education, which resulted in a new document entitled, *Achieving excellence: A renewed vision for Ontario* (Ontario Ministry of Education, 2014). It contained four main goals: achieving excellence (which referred to literacy, numeracy, high school graduation); equity (which involved reducing the gap between subgroups); promoting well-being (positive sense of self and belonging); and enhancing public confidence in the public education system. In other words, the agenda was the same as before with the significant addition of equity and well-being.

During 2013 I never asked myself the question of whether I was still advisor or not. When it came time to be clear Premier Wynne wanted four advisors: Jean Clinton (a child psychiatrist and neuroscientist), Carol Campbell (who I had recruited in 2005, and was now at OISE), Andy Hargreaves, and me. I was a bit surprised that Premier Wynne wanted me because when she was Minister and I was with Dalton, we were not totally aligned. She thought literacy numeracy was too narrow, and we in the Premier's office were concerned that well-being at the time was too diffuse, and furthermore that increased academic success including closing the gap would go a long way to achieving greater equity. The whole matter of the relationship between success in learning, equity, and well-being is critical, but I will defer this question until the final section of this chapter so that we won't get ahead of ourselves. I can say that as of September 2017 in Ontario we are pretty much agreed on the core agenda. I'll give the details in the Deep Learning section of this chapter.

California Dreaming

I knew from *No Child Left Behind* (NCLB), signed by President George W Bush on January 8, 2002, that the US was in trouble. *Race to the Top* (RTTT) was not much better. No matter how you look at it the US is a wrong driver country and I said so in the 'wrong drivers' paper. But I also knew that there were a lot of 'right driver' people working under the radar in places like California where we were doing some work, and had known some very highly effective schools districts. As Sahlberg (2018) points out, many of the best and most effective ideas came from US research such as: cooperative learning, collaboration among teachers, teachers and students learning together, constructivism, and more. Governor Jerry Brown in California was moving toward a new form of decentralization of resources called Local Control Funding Formula (LCFF), and its companion the Local Control Accountability Plan (LCAP). An influential group consisting of ten mostly large districts formed a consortium called CORE (California Office to Reform Education) applied for and received a Federal Waiver with respect to NCLB using the 'wrong drivers' paper as its model. In short, there was a lot of potential affinity between the Ontario approach and what California aspired to.

The Stuart Foundation based in San Francisco and devoted to social improvement took notice. In partnership with us, Stuart funded three delegations of 40 or so leaders in each group to conduct study visits to Ontario, which took place in 2014 and 2015. The state superintendent, president of the teachers union, several leading district superintendents, and others spent four days at a time in Toronto and the surrounding area examining our policies and practices. Essentially the visitors concluded that they wanted to implement a California version of the Ontario strategy. The Stuart Foundation funded us with a three-year grant (2014 to 2017, and now being extended beyond 2017) to support and keep track of the evolution of LCFF. We just completed an audit or stock taking of the state of LCFF/LCAP (*California's Golden Opportunity: Taking Stock: Leadership from the Middle*; see Fullan & Rincón-Gallardo, 2016, www.michaelfullan.ca). California is a complex case: 6.2 million students, over 1000 districts, 58 counties. All in all California consists of multi-layers with huge diversity and poverty.

In our 'taking stock' report we found that LCFF/LCAP is on the right track, has widespread support, but requires much greater capacity building than was thought to be necessary. Success will also require greater leadership at the school district, and county levels, more intense focus, and more investment in the teaching profession of the kind that Linda Darling Hammond is working on in California and elsewhere.

As for the purpose of this book—identifying significant ideas that I am associated with at particular points in history—the timing could not be more crucial for the US. I am proud to be connected to California which sees itself leading the country in education for diversity, immigration, climate change, and the like. In short, the ideas that we built over the last two decades are taking us into more and more exciting and critical arenas of transformation. I think I know a lot and have significant ideas to contribute, but I am more attracted to learning more by helping to figure out with local leaders how to improve a situation as complex and as critical as is California and the country in which it sits. By this time, moral purpose with complexity had become the turn on for me.

My Love Affair with Practitioners

I feel I should now update who was on our team; what else we were doing; and what I was writing around 2013 and following. I was working closely with Joanne Quinn who had started with me as the district rep from Halton in the Learning Consortium in 1988. Thereafter I had enabled her secondment to the Ontario government, then hired her as head of continuing education at the new OISE/UT where she took a low level performing unit to a high profit enterprise, always a treat for a Dean. Then in 2004 she joined the freelance consulting world and has worked with me since on system capacity building in California and elsewhere. Our 2016 book, *Coherence: The right drivers in action for schools, districts, and systems* (Fullan & Quinn, 2016), in many ways came from our workshops in California and is a blockbuster seller with some 40,000 copies sold since its appearance.

Claudia Cuttress became my mainstay technical support system providing the graphics and feed in for the hundreds of workshops and consultancies we did, as well as establishing and developing our website.

Claudia knows our work inside out, and it shows. By a stroke of luck in January 2013 I stumbled on one of the greatest young academics around—Santiago Rincón-Gallardo. Santiago had come via Mexico to do his doctorate with Richard Elmore at Harvard, one of the greatest school improvement scholars in the world. Santiago met his to be wife, Asha who was also at Harvard, and fortunately (for us) was from Toronto. They moved to Toronto and in January 2013 I met with Santiago in the lobby of OISE and within 12 minutes offered him a job of Chief Researcher in our group. Santiago and I had discussions about his future. The gist of it was: you could become an assistant professor, and work your way up, or you could come and work with me, jump start academia, and then write your own ticket as an academic five years hence. We both knew that applied work, John Dewey, Kurt Lewin, Paulo Freire et al., and our modern work would run rings around the slow pace of overburdened assistant professors. In four years, Santiago has produced, with and without me, a heap of great work. He can indeed write his own ticket, but luckily is not yet inclined to do so. And when he does move he will always be a great partner in school and system improvement.

A group of practitioners make the majority of our team (80% of your best ideas come from your leading customers). In addition to Joanne Quinn there is Eleanor Adam, who was also from Halton, and serves as a designer and trainer for a lot of our work in California. Bill Hogarth, the super successful Director of York Region District School Board, is part of our group. York Region just named a secondary school after him: Bill Hogarth Secondary School. Mary Jean Gallagher finished her term as head of LNS and now does system consulting with me, and on her own in California, Australia, and Latin America. We are writing *The devil is in the details* book together. Joelle Rodway, a doctoral graduate from OISE specializing in social networks, works with us as a researcher. Terry Jakobsmeier is our talented multi-purpose accountant who always keeps us in the black. We have a host of people working in deep learning that I will get to later in this section.

I was also getting involved in other big issues that came to have special meaning for me, once I got close to them. One involves Quebec; the other the First Nations, Métis, Inuit (FNMI). Quebec is one of the high performing provinces in Canada, but its school districts wanted to proceed more explicitly to higher and more equitable levels of performance. Historically there has not been much operational connection between Quebec and other provinces at the level of practice because of cultural and language differences. In 2014 the Chagnon Foundation based in Montreal wanted to address the gaps in achievement. Its President, Claude Chagnon, wrote "we refuse to accept the inevitably of poverty. In a society such as ours, it is unacceptable that many, many children are still living and growing up in disadvantaged conditions". The Foundation invited me to meet with some Quebec directors of education in 2015, and we quickly worked out a strategy that Andy Hargreaves had identified as a strength of Ontario that he called 'leadership from the middle' (essentially school districts playing a greater role in system development by becoming stronger themselves). In 2015 the Chagnon Foundation employed a respected retired Director of Education, Claude St Cyr, to lead the initiative, and hired me as a consultant to Claude. We are now intensely involved in implementation. The group—Chagnon and the directors—have now published two of my books en francais: *Le leadership moteur* (*Motion leadership*) and *Coherence* (and are about to translate our new book on 'Deep Learning'). For me as an English Canadian working on system change in Quebec it is a deeply emotional experience as well as a good challenge at system change. Quebec is already a very good system, similar in performance to Ontario. We expect it to get even better in the next three years including gains in deeper learning.

You can't be a Canadian without being embarrassed and heartbroken at the tragic history and abuse of FNMI peoples. *A Truth and Reconciliation Commission* reported in 2016 what every Canadian should know—that in the first 150 years of Canada (since 1867, and before) FNMI children were ripped from their families, placed into residential schools only to be abused. The current federal government has committed to acting on the matter, but so far, after two years, little concrete action has been taken. The matter is complicated because education is the purview of each province and territory, except for First Nations peoples living on reserves, which is a federal responsibility. Fundamental living conditions represent one set of problems, but education is the long-term solution. Our team is committed to helping and has carried out one small project. We are seeking an opportunity to work with indigenous education leaders to do something concrete in the area of education development—to learn from them as well as to work with them. In working with different cultures, especially ones that have been ignored and mistreated, it is crucial that you enter with a stance about what you *don't know*. Learning from lead practitioners is especially important with cultures that might have a lot to teach us—like the Maori in New Zealand, and the FNMI in Canada. Two-way learning partnerships with FNMI are essential for Canada's next stage of development.

The Deep Learning Revolution

During 2013–2014 I was doing what I call reading the tea leaves. I had written the short 'Achieving excellence' paper for Dalton. I had identified focused innovation around the 6Cs as promising goals. I began to see data that showed that students were increasingly disengaged as they moved up the grade levels. I noticed schools that were exceptions to the norm like Park Manor in Elmira, Ontario with its principal, James Bond, whom I had featured in 'the skinny' and whose teachers were using technology and getting impressive results. But I did not know much about technology. So I did the best fastest thing: in the summer of 2012 I blitz read about 50 books on technology, so that I could write *my own* book on the topic (writing being one of my two best ways of learning; the other is 'doing').

The result was *Stratosphere: Integrating technology, pedagogy, and change knowledge* (2013c). I basically concluded that these three forces were on the move but not connected. Technology was the race leader, but helter-skelter. Pedagogy was now establishing itself thanks to our work in Ontario, and to John Hattie's visible learning (which, while requires careful interpretation, has put pedagogy in the center of the debate). The third component, change knowledge—how to lead and participate in complex change—was coming to the fore via the group of us working on coping with and leading change. I observed that these three forces needed each other but so far they were going their separate ways.

On the way to deep learning I wrote two more books, *The principal: Three keys to maximizing impact* (2014c), and the fifth edition of *The new meaning of educational change* (2016b). The principal book was especially significant. In the early 2000s some policy makers at the district and state levels picked up the research that seemed to say that school principals who are instructional leaders are most effective.

Accordingly they went to town on the matter. Job descriptions were re-written to stress instructional focus; criteria for appointment got altered; principals were given checklists, and required to engage in walkthroughs (sometimes these were tied to teacher evaluation); and supervisors at the district level were expected to monitor principals on the job to make sure they were carrying out their new roles. I called the whole thing 'micro-management madness'. I knew there was something wrong because the good principals I knew faked it. They did not want to ruin their relationships with teachers.

Then I went to the research: Ken Leithwood, Viviane Robinson, et al. What they actually found was different. Effective principals 'participated as learners' with teachers in helping the school move forward. They made sure the focus was on pedagogy linked to student engagement and achievement. They 'used the group to change the group'. They influenced learning alright, but they did so indirectly, but nonetheless explicitly *through* the group. I then was able to redefine the principals' role in terms of three impacts: be a lead learner, be a system player (go outside to contribute to the system as you come back inside to improve your school), and be a change agent (learn how to work with both push and pull). My publisher, in this case Jossey-Bass, told me that the book was flying off the shelves. I had captured the principals' reality as if I were in their shoes: their negative shoes if they were being micro-managed, and positive shoes if they were learning and leveraging with the group. I pursued the themes of coherence and sustainability in a small book called, *Indelible leadership: Always leave them learning* (2016a) in which I concluded that the main role of leaders is to build collaborative cultures to the point where the leader becomes *dispensable*. The best legacy any leader can have is to leave the group with the capacity to carry on without him or her; indeed, to go deeper and further.

Two more seminal change ideas came out of the two books just mentioned. One referred to being a lead learner with the group, and is expressed as: 'if you want to change the group use the group to change the group'.

Seminal Idea #11: Be a lead learner and use the group to change the group.

The other idea concerned the need to build a focused collaborative culture not only to have greater impact through 'collective efficacy', but also to leave as your main legacy a culture that can carry on after you have left. It is expressed as follows:

Seminal Idea #12: As a leader, develop a collaborative culture of other leaders over a five to six-year period to the point where you become dispensable.

Increasingly since 2013, all of these events, and the education world as it was evolving (or should we say more accurately not evolving), made me more receptive to something big. As usual the opportunity knocked on my door and in a strange way dragged me out into the bigger world. I had worked for the previous decade off and on with Greg Butler, the Australian who had built a career with Microsoft leading their high profile 'Partners in Learning' (PiL) program where each country in the world had a PiL Microsoft leader whose job it was to foster relationships with the education sector within the country.

Greg left Microsoft in 2013 and contacted me to discuss his next big idea. I knew him quite well. His notion was to create a living laboratory around the world where *systems* (clusters of schools) in different countries would develop and share radically new learning geared toward a complex future. He obtained seed money from Microsoft, Intel, Promethean, and others. The idea would be to recruit about 100 schools from each of ten countries for this 1000-school venture. He had his own ideas. Greg was also stimulated by the ideas in my book *Stratosphere*. Michael Barber, who was then with Pearson, had started a 'thought series' on important topics of the day and he agreed to fund a major report on 'deep learning'. Maria Langworthy (freelance Microsoft researcher) and I teamed up and wrote a report called *A rich seam: How new pedagogies find deep learning* (2014) that provided a lot of the framework and evidence that deep learning was the way to go. Greg invited Joanne Quinn and me to join his group that included Joanne McEachen and others in Seattle to launch the New Pedagogies for Deep Learning (NPDL) global network. I never would have initiated anything so bold as what Greg had in mind.

At the first meetings country groups began to sign on: Australia, Canada, Finland, Netherlands, Uruguay; later New Zealand and the US joined. In some countries it was governments that made the decision to join (Victoria, Australia, Finland (along with key municipalities), and Uruguay), while in other countries it was local groups such as school districts or networks (Canada, New Zealand, US).

New pedagogies were defined in terms of new learning partnerships between and among students, teachers, and parents; deep learning was the 6Cs. At the front end Greg, Joanne Quinn, and Joanne McEachen developed a set of tools and protocols that further operationalized the 6Cs, the new pedagogies, school conditions, cluster and system factors. I was happy with this arrangement because Greg ran the project within his company, and we were external partners. As we moved forward, Greg was attending the annual Bett meeting in London in January 2015. Bett is the highest profile technology-education convention in the world. I was scheduled to join Greg later that week.

Early Sunday morning, January 18, 2015, at the age of 57, Greg committed suicide by jumping into the pathway of an incoming train—a London Tube car. Here was Greg at a convention that he had cut his teeth on, in a city of nine million people. At 6am on that Sunday morning, surrounded by abstract hordes of people, Greg must have been the loneliest man in the world. It hit me hard. I knew Greg had suffered with depression from time to time, but it was not noticeable. He was always upbeat and optimistic, inspiring to work with—a generous, lovely person.

A month later we had to decide what to do. We consulted with our cluster leaders from the five countries that were members. To a person, to a group the resounding response was that we must continue. In the summer of 2015 we relocated NPDL to Toronto to be led by Joanne Quinn, Joanne McEachen, and me. Greg and I had secured a 1.5 million dollar grant from the Hewlett Foundation (a foundation devoted to promoting deep learning). The education director of Hewlett, Barbara Chow, moved a couple of small mountains to transfer the money to us—a difficult feat because we were a Canadian entity being funded by a US Foundation with only one of seven countries based in the US. We would not have been able to continue if it were not for Barbara.

We had a strong framework for pursuing deep learning, but we were entering brand new territory, at least on the scale we were attempting. We were, together with our country partners, trying to invent the future of public education. We had made it clear that we wanted clusters to join us, not because they wanted part of somebody else's global adventure, but rather because they saw in us a direction that they wanted to go in anyway. We wanted them *to exploit NPDL in order to explore and develop a direction that they valued.*

What has happened since the fall of 2015, a little over two years, is phenomenal. I will describe some of the essence of this work here, but the full story up to this point is contained in our book *Deep learning: Engage the world Change the world* that has just been released by Corwin (2018).

We can capture the story by discussing: what is the essence of deep learning; what transpired when we enacted it collectively in the seven countries, especially what were the surprises; and where does it fit in today's and tomorrow's world? I draw the responses to these three questions from our *Engage the world* book. Finally, we can catch up to Ontario the week of September 5–8 when it made some startling policy announcements even to me, and I was around the table.

In deep learning there is the push factor and the pull factor. The push factor is that traditional schooling is boring, and for some fundamentally alienating, as you go up the grade levels. Schooling is an institution that is increasingly unfit for the purposes society now faces. This is not so much a criticism as it is a fact of evolutionary life. Schooling does not give us what we need to live effectively these days. One could even ask the rhetorical question, 'is it possible for a student to get good grades' and still not be fit for life in 2018 and beyond? The big push factor to sum up is 'there is no reason for the majority of students to take conventional schooling seriously'. The pull factors are powerful and amorphous. They include what we refer to as the siren call of technology—an ever-alluring mixture of escapism and absorption in open-ended learning. The other absolutely fundamental draw is new learning that almost obliterates the distinction between schooling and living (this is very much what John Dewey had in mind over 100 years ago when he said: "education is not preparation for life, it is life itself").

Our approach to deep learning, building on the start up with Greg, is to work with clusters of schools in order to enact and create a radically new form of learning. The essence of our framework consists of five interrelated factors. First, we focus on the 6Cs: character, citizenship, collaboration, communication, creativity, and critical thinking. We see these as learning outcomes, as well as forming the basis of educational experiences. Second, we buttress the 6Cs with what we call 'four pillars of learning': engaging pedagogical practices; learning partnerships between and among students, teachers and families; re-design of learning environments; and leveraging digital. Third, we support the development of school conditions (primarily focused collaboration well-led) that foster deep learning as the core goal. Fourth, we work with local cluster leaders and district/municipalities to help them coordinate and stimulate deep learning in the schools. Fifth and finally, we examine and try to influence broader infrastructure conditions at the policy level. All five of these components are infused with *collaborative inquiry* through which we 'cause' change and learn how to improve it.

If you ask what has happened since 2014 the general answer is 'plenty'—some of which is downright astonishing. Our book, *Engage the world*, contains numerous specific examples, so I will only supply the highlights here.

Deep learning is quality learning that *sticks*. Among other things, deep learning:

1 Develops self and others' expectations for more learning and achievement.
2 Increases student engagement in the learning through personalization and ownership.
3 Connects students to the 'real world' reflective of their own reality and cultural identity.
4 Resonates with spiritual values that connect to vast numbers of the population whether secular or religious.
5 Builds skills, knowledge, self-confidence, and self-efficacy through inquiry.
6 Fosters new relationships with and between the learner, their family, their communities, and their teachers.
7 Deepens human desire to connect with others to do good.

(Fullan, Quinn and McEachen, 2018, p. 9)

Deep learning basically brings the 6Cs alive, and fundamentally alters the nature of learning as it shapes the outcomes learners take into society. In the course of the work we experienced a number of *discoveries* (and that is the most accurate word) that were not in our learning design but now seem inevitable once you unleash what learners and leaders can do. There were six big surprises—themes that emerged through our deep learning work with the seven countries:

1 *Helping humanity:* Children and youth have a natural affinity to improving humanity.
2 *Life and learning merge:* Learning is most powerful when it is closest to what is important in daily life.
3 *Working with others is an intrinsic motivator:* Doing something of value with others is a deeply human experience.
4 *Character, citizenship, and creativity are catalytic Cs:* These are the drivers of comprehensive action to discover and make valuable things happen.
5 *Young people are the best change agents:* Babies onward, but not in isolation. Young and older people need each other: discover the synergy.
6 *Attack inequity with excellence:* As the world gets more unequal, the power of deep learning to achieve greater excellence with disconnected students becomes crucial for the survival of the planet.

(Fullan, Quinn and McEachen, 2018, p. 164)

These are remarkable because they are organic or natural as you create conditions for more meaningful learning, where individual and societal values develop in unison. Instead of focusing on remedial work for those who were not keeping up, we saw expectations rise and be exceeded, and we identified that learning could be accelerated—when people are doing something meaningful with others, and that something has impact, they can't wait to do more.

This didn't happened everywhere or for all students, but it happened enough, and when supported it spread quickly. We now believe that it has potential to become widespread which is a formidable challenge to say the least. When we wrote about our equity hypothesis (attack equity with excellence: don't dumb down, smarten up) in another paper one of our reviewers, Richard Elmore, was skeptical about the argument. He had written an article in 1995 titled 'Getting to scale with good education practice'. Now he told us:

"Institutionalized thinking tends to project the future in ways that are compatible with the preservation of existing, predictable structures". He proceeded to say, "we can talk about 'systems' as much as we want, [but that] "society is increasingly morphing into something much less rigidly defined and much more lateral and networked".

(personal communication, 2017)

In short, he was saying it is futile to try to change the existing schools system; and besides, Elmore intimates, that societal forces (technology, networks, chaos, and so on) will rip the status quo apart in any case. He may turn out to be right, but my view is that if this is the case, survivors will be better off if they have learned deeply with our 6Cs.

Meanwhile, something interesting was happening in Ontario. I implied earlier that the four advisors (Campbell, Clinton, Hargreaves, and me) were having a running conversation with our bosses over the past year about the relationship between equity and learning. The Premier, Kathleen Wynne, and the Minister, Mitzie Hunter, were insistent that equity was to be the top priority. I respected that because I felt that we did not do enough in that area in the 2004–2010 period. But some of us also argued that the equity agenda and the learning agenda were both required, and indeed that you could not get very far with one if the other was not also incorporated. On June 14, 2017, we had a major all day meeting with the Premier, Minister, and (unusual for our meeting) there was a cast of some 20 other policy people in the session. We again had the discussion about the need to link learning and equity if the latter were to be achieved. It was a fuller and more substantial meeting than normal.

I was encouraged about the quality of the debate, but did not think much beyond it. The plan was that the politicians and ministry staff would work over the summer to further develop the ideas that were scheduled for a series of announcements the first week of school (September 4–7). As it turned out there were four main announcements that week. To say that I was gobsmacked would be an understatement. Yes, there was a strong equity action plan (Ontario Ministry of Education, 2017). Yes, there was to be a curriculum review including math. But two other related fundamental actions were included. The Ontario report card would be revamped to focus on six 'transferable skills': "critical thinking, innovation and creativity, self-directed learning, collaboration, communication, and citizenship". These were of course the 6Cs with one substitution: Self-directed learning for character (not a bad change since character was about self-efficacy and action). The fourth policy proposal was that the province would re-examine assessing student learning in the context of the assessment agency, the EQAO. The review would focus on student assessment relative to equity and learning including the transferable skills. Carol Campbell was appointed to lead the review with the advisors (there had been two advisors added recently; Carl James, a sociologist from York University, and Diane Longboat representing the FNMI communities, bringing the total to six of us).

The set of proposals represented a stunning development. In *A rich seam*, Maria Langworthy and I had found many local examples of deep learning, but we stressed that local innovators found that the greatest obstacles they faced were systemic barriers—policies and practices at the infrastructure level. We concluded that *no system in the world* had what was needed at the policy level to accomplish whole system deep learning (including Singapore that I will reference in the Postscript). Now Ontario seemed to be doing just that—providing substantial system direction and support. It is important to note that these developments are at the proposal stage. A lot can happen to alter the scenario on the way to actual policy acceptance and implementation. But to me they are part of the inevitable trend toward transformation of the public school system with which I have been engaged for the past two decades.

With the potential new policies in, and with the considerable work on the ground across the 72 districts, and the 4900 schools, Ontario is now positioned to 'put it all together'. There are many districts in the province working with us to implement the 6Cs and related aspects, actions that preceded the new policies. Now that the pieces are converging it is still necessary to point out that these accomplishments are fragile. There will be a provincial election in June 2018, and the current Premier currently has a low rating in the polls. I must say her response to the low ratings has been interesting. As she put it "you don't have to like me, but love my policies". What's not to love in education? The recent education polices, and the appetite for deep implementation, are very strong in Ontario at all levels. It has taken a decade and a half to get to this level of quality and system depth, and it probably has the solidity to persist into the future.

I hope it is clear I am not claiming that I 'caused' these latest changes. There were others pushing for the solution that occurred. This is a professional autobiography about critical change developments that I was associated with and helped shape. Changes of this magnitude and depth require support from many quarters, and I have been fortunate enough to be connected with several of the key players, especially over the past decade and a half. To grow up in Ontario and in Canada at this particular time in history has put me in the right place at the right time. Lucky me. Sometimes luck develops the mind; and then it favors the prepared mind.

POSTSCRIPT:
STILL SURREAL

It is January 1, 2018 as I pen these words. You have probably guessed that *Nuance* and the *Devil* have taken a back seat—more accurately a side seat—to this book. Once I started *Surreal* I couldn't stop. I am guessing that the other two books will be better off because of this detour, and will be completed within a year. As we close I would like to visit the following. What else is happening on the global scene with respect to educational development? Let's collect the 12 seminal ideas in one place. Where do my ideas come from anyway? How do I write? And, why is education so crucial for the future of the world?

The Global Scene

This is not a book intended to cover the field, but only to chronicle and capture the ideas that I have been associated with. In this respect I have had the fortune to grow up in a time where *system change* (the transformation of educational systems for the betterment of students and society) has come to the fore. In this respect we are at a transition point: partly because the work of the past decade is coming to fruition; and partly because the problems have become more complex with the technical and social chaos, and opportunities that abound. There seem to be two main groups working on system change in education, which themselves are not internally homogenous but can serve as a contemporary reference point. I know and work with most of the people involved. One I am going to call the PISA crowd; the other, and smaller, upstart shall we say, is ARC—the Atlantic Rim Collaboratory founded by Andy Hargreaves and his colleagues (see below).

The PISA crowd concerns the work of OECD (the western founded Organization of Economic Cooperation and Development) that has developed the Programme for International Student Assessment (PISA), which among other things has been assessing the performance of 15-year-olds in a growing number of countries (some 90 at present) focusing on literacy, math, and science. PISA, led by its Education Director, Andreas Schleicher, has conducted assessments of large numbers of students every three years since the year 2000 (six assessments so far), and has been formulating policy recommendations accordingly. PISA assesses excellence (academic performance) and equity (the size of the gap between high and low performers). In the latest round the countries performing in the so-called golden quadrant (high performance/high equity) are Canada, Estonia, Hong Kong (China), and Macau (China). PISA continues to evolve as it enters the arena to assess 'collaborative problem solving' and 'global competencies' (Schleicher, in press).

These developments are quite complicated and beyond the scope of this book to go into detail about. There are several new books that are attempting to sort some of this out: critiques by Pasi Sahlberg's *FinnishED leadership* (2018), and Dennis Shirley's *The new imperatives of educational change: Achievement with integrity* (2017), as well as Andreas Schleicher's forthcoming book, *Worldclass*. A few of the main issues relative to my quest represented in the previous chapters of this book include: the overemphasis on tests, even good ones like PISA's; the failure to get at well-being; taking PISA too literally; and in the case of the US ignoring external data. Our group in deep learning is working with Andreas et al. on their development of newer measures akin to the 6Cs. OECD because of its official political base tends to move slowly. My main message is do not judge PISA or ARC as internally homogenous groups. Both groups are investigating complex matters, and considering various alternatives.

Of special interest is Singapore because it has been a top performer on PISA since the assessments began. It is a small country with only about 350 schools. The best inside story of the nature of Singapore's development and current state is the book *Learning from Singapore* in this Routledge series, just published by Pak Tee Ng (2017), the

Associate Director, Leadership, of the National Institute of Education. We find out the main reason that Singapore has been successful: universal emphasis on education; development of leadership for virtually all educators in the system; strong and systematic professional capital, great curriculum, emphasizing 'less is more'; deepening knowledge base, and more (see also Shirley's 2017 account). But Pak Tee as an insider identifies perennial tensions or paradoxes such as: how to combine merit and equity; coordinating centralization and decentralization; timely vs timelessness of change; and how to manage 'teach less, learn more'. In other words, the key issues involve dilemmas and require constant attention, and analysis.

South Korea and China (especially Shanghai) are top performers in PISA, but on closer inspection the extreme competition and stress may be taking its toll. Speaking of autobiographies there is a fascinating account by a Chinese American mother who returned to China and enrolled her 3-year-old son in an elite Shanghai school (Chu, 2017). The title of the book, *Little soldiers*, tells you a lot about Chu's initial experiences, but Chu also identifies increasing cracks in the Chinese 'culture of obedience' at schools arising from pressures coming from an increasingly large middle class, and indeed from some Chinese leaders themselves who realize that fostering greater creativity in schools will be essential for the future of the country.

In all these cases my point is that the situations are not as straightforward as they seem, which is another way of saying you need the change-related seminal ideas and qualities that I have experienced and identified in order to cope with the dynamics of system change.

Another source of inspiration is the ARC group—again, I know and interact with the players. The ARC was founded in 2015 by Andy Hargreaves and some colleagues. There are currently ten members: the Ministries of Scotland, Iceland, Ireland, Finland, Aruba, the province of Ontario, Sweden, the US states of California and Vermont, and Wales. The group's self proclaimed vision and mission is:

> To establish education systems that advance equity, excellence, wellbeing, inclusion, democracy and human rights for all students within high-quality professionally–run systems. In a world of disruptive economic transformations, growing inequalities and rapid change, it is important to

broaden and deepen our approach to how we interpret and improve high quality educational systems for all our students.

(ARC, 2017)

In summary, one could conclude that there are a number of prominent players milling around in the same domain. In many ways Ontario is reflective of the journey: how to obtain system wide equity and excellence with deep learning that is required for a complex world in flux.

There is one more coincidence that is personal to me, and seems random unless you believe in surrealism. My middle child, Josh, who is now 44 years of age, started his career as a secondary school teacher and now leads a worldwide enterprise called Maximum City (MC; 2017). Essentially MC organizes groups of students who work on various initiatives that identify significant urban problems, study them, and present their findings and proposed remedies to a panel of industry professionals. The program is award winning, has expanded rapidly, and currently operates in three countries: Canada (Ontario), China, and Germany. It is deep learning in spades. I have had nothing to do with the origin and development of the program (unless you believe in DNA), although Josh and I have plenty to talk about these days on this front. Josh's mother Sylvia, a secondary school science teacher, also had a lot to do with his earlier development.

My overall points in this section are: there is a lot going on worldwide; it is a contentious field; it is out in the open, and it augurs well for deeper work on system change. I have been in on the ground floor since 2003, and we can expect accelerated attention to this domain in the next five years and more. I can say flat out that we are at the beginning of a period of radical transformation of public education and schooling of the likes that we have never before witnessed: radical, unpredictable, wonderful, and dangerous. Because of powerful internal and external to the system forces, it is a dead certainty that fundamental changes will be visited upon us. Basic changes at the system or policy level will finally start to occur as we see in present day Ontario, New Zealand (recently), Singapore, and soon, China as well as others who will join. When the Berlin wall falls it falls rapidly. Although new alternatives often take a while to evolve, this time that too will be different—rapid new patterns will form and disseminate at new speeds with mutual multi-way knock on effects.

My personal and professional interests at this point include: Canada (including FNMI, and all provinces and territories); the US, especially California; the seven DL countries (Australia, Canada, Finland, Netherlands, New Zealand, Uruguay, and the US); Latin America (in addition to Uruguay we have some involvement in Argentina, Chile, Colombia, Mexico, Peru); OECD related work in several countries; and a potentially growing interest in South Korea, and China where they have translated many of my books into mandarin, and claim to be using the ideas. I have little direct involvement in two of the largest entities: the continent of Africa and India—or Pakistan (although the village sign quoting me that I mentioned at the beginning was in a remote village in northern Pakistan).

The 12 Seminal Ideas

There are 12 seminal ideas dispersed throughout the book. They are all very close to action, and virtually all have been generated through my journey of working toward system change in increasingly larger and more complex contexts. I consider many of them to be in the category of *sticky* insights, which means not only good ideas, but also ones that stay with you because they have a vivid, memorable way of putting something. I will return to the notion of sticky in the next section related to where my ideas come from.

Seminal Idea #1:	*Implementation is the sine qua non of educational change.*
Seminal Idea #2:	*At the heart of educational change is personal and collective meaning.*
Seminal Idea #3:	*All real change is action oriented.*
Seminal Idea #4:	*Be as assertive as you can get away with; including the kicker, but only if they thank you afterward.*
Seminal Idea #5:	*A leader is only as good as the team she/he builds and interacts with. Trust and interact is the key to mutual efficacy.*
Seminal Idea #6:	*My ideas come from a mixture of doing change, reading, and writing.*
Seminal Idea #7:	*When you are in conflict with someone who has good ideas, and good values, build don't burn bridges.*

Seminal Idea #8:   *Autonomy is not isolation. You need collaboration to be effective autonomously, and vice versa. Collaborative professionalism honors both the individual and the collective. (And a nod to Andy's and my breakthrough idea—the professional capital of teachers)*

Seminal Idea #9:   *Eighty percent of your best ideas come from your leading customers.*

Seminal Idea #10:   *Successful change processes are a function of shaping and reshaping good ideas they build capacity and ownership.*

Seminal Idea #11:   *Be a lead learner and use the group to change the group.*

Seminal Idea #12:   *As a leader, develop a collaborative culture of other leaders over a five to six-year period to the point where you become dispensable.*

Where Do My Ideas Come From?

In Seminal Idea #6 I said that my ideas come from doing, reading, and writing, but that is a general answer. Another answer, still general but truthful, is that I don't really know. But I owe it to the reader to probe more deeply. In an abstract mysterious way I think the ideas come from the interaction of my subconscious and the surreal world. Definitions of the subconscious define it variously as 'the totality of mental processes of which the individual is not aware'; or, 'in the mind but not immediately available'. Some of these hidden sources are long standing, and presumably are stimulated by new experiences that might connect in unknown but valuable (or dysfunctional) ways. I am a firm believer in evolution, namely that good patterns are more likely to be retained over time.

Interestingly, one of Pasi Sahlberg's doctoral students, Raisa Ahtiainen, did her Ph.D dissertation (which she successfully defended September 8, 2017) comparing mine and Andy Hargreaves' works. The title: 'Shades of change in Fullan's and Hargreaves's models' (Ahtiainen, 2017). I won't review her findings but one thing she concluded about me rings true. Raisa claims that my pre-2010 writing reflected the 'overwhelmingness' and chaotic nature of change, and that my approach in 2010 is different.

> Things are still complex, but now they have been approached in a manner that is clearer, perhaps more practice oriented and not so desperate. Thus ... factors related to managing and confronting change seemed to become simpler, yet the change remains demanding.
>
> *(p.129)*

My ideas came from the interaction of what was in me (ever evolving), and my need to make a connection with those doing change. My goal, although I never stated it this way, was to be insightful in a way that practitioners would find dead-on about their situations, but would never have stated it that way themselves. In a way, I gave them 'sticky language' that would stimulate action that they controlled and that would stay with them. When I created the phrase 'use the group to change the group' leaders knew instantly what I meant, and it gave them license and ways of acting. When I said create a collaborative culture that over time makes you dispensable, people got it. Adapting Robinson's (2011) finding, that effective principals 'participate as learners' with teachers in order to move the school forward, it stayed with people. And so on.

I would take on writing certain books in order to get new insights. *Stratosphere* (2013c) gave me 'pedagogy is the driver, technology is the accelerator'. One of my most stimulating (for me) books was one where I ventured into the realm of personal change in a book entitled, *Freedom to change* (2015). I was noticing in our work that people were willing to put a lot of energy into getting rid of constraints, but when successful were not so good at handling the new opportunities. It immediately reminded me, a bit vaguely until I checked, of my old sociology days, and a classic book by the psychoanalyst Eric Fromm, *Escape from freedom* (1969, 2nd edition). This led to a host of insights. People could get mobilized against things they did not like, but were less focused about what to do next. It led me to understand feedback: focus on the receiver, not the giver, and its corollary: 'combine candor with autonomy'. Yes, Bruce Joyce was half right. Candor is essential, but people need leeway to process it and infuse their own meaning. Finally, my insights about 'wrong drivers' were amplified. Originally in 2011 I showed how certain wrong policy drivers such as punitive accountability and individualistic solutions were ineffective or worse, and I named the alternatives: transparency of evidence combined with non-judgmentalism, and teamwork and other forms of collaboration that led to collective efficacy. But I failed to realize that people would not necessarily be good at the new ways of working. Now I have a new insight that we are putting into practice in California: how to address the problem of 'superficial implementation of the right drivers'. How do we liberate groups of learners and still get effective 'system change'? And, so it goes.

How Do I Write My Books?

How do I write books? My immersion in doing (consulting), leading workshops, and reading widely gives me ideas. Insights emerge when I see a particularly good practice, or read a gem of a book (one or two seem to come along exactly as I need them). Sticky phrases occur to me as you can see from the title of my books: *The meaning of change; All systems go; Stratosphere; Motion leadership; The six secrets, Coherence; Engage the world*, and the soon to be famous, *Nuance*, and *The devil* (just kidding; they are not written yet—incidentally I am breaking my cardinal rule—never talk publicly about a book before it is written. I hope I am not courting bad luck.). I read, ruminate, and rummage through good practice. After months of gestation, and seemingly suddenly, I know when I am ready to write. I write quickly—a chapter every day or two with interim, dreamy like lulls of one or a few days. The subconscious does its work. Magically the book comes together. During this period I am inattentive to other matters—borderline inaccessible. I wrote this autobiography in three weeks. Then a few second thoughts, new thoughts, feedback from my publisher and reviewers, and voila!

Why is Education Crucial to the Future of the World?

We need a specific answer not a general one to this question. It takes us back to the heart of deep learning. The answer I believe is embedded in what Brazilian educator Paulo Freire worked on with peasants in the 1960s. At the time Freire made this profound observation: humankind's main 'vocation' he said, is as a subject "who acts upon, and transforms the world, and in so doing moves toward ever new possibilities of a fuller and richer life individually and collectively" (Freire, 2000, p. 32). All of our work in deep learning tells us that this is the way to go, that it is practical and possible to accomplish, albeit devilishly hard to do. You can only deeply learn if you 'engage the world' and in so doing you change yourself, *and* the world for the better. How is that for a mission statement! The saving grace is that the journey is incredibly motivational to join. In our *Deep learning: Engage the world Change the world*, we see that hordes of students want to learn things that are meaningful and that serve personal and collective moral purposes.

On balance, things are stacked against the possibility of transforming the status quo in the way I am talking about: growing inequality and in many cases structural and blatant racism; a chaotic and unpredictable employment future; spontaneous networks that are easily mobilized for evil, and so on. Things could easily go horribly wrong. But make no mistake, radical change will be increasingly upon us. We have a choice of being a passive casualty (and in some cases a temporary lucky beneficiary) but it will be the deep learners that create and thus inherit a better world.

When you shift the emphasis to what is possible, and potentially up to the challenge it always takes you back to education—a certain kind of education. This has been the journey of the last 50 years for me; not a planned one but one that drew me in to the point that I was influencing as much as being influenced. Education of the kind I am talking about is humankind's *ultimate freedom*. It serves the person and the group in a highly specific and motivating manner that gets at identity and purpose. It creates citizens of tomorrow, in the here and now of today.

I can't think of a more powerful change force than mobilizing and unleashing hordes of young people who become agents of change as a function of how and what they learn (we have not yet found the lower age limit of students as forces for change). It can't be a small force in a few schools. It has to be the mandate of the many. There are many children in desperate circumstances in both developed and developing countries. They need to be helped to get above a minimum survival threshold. As they do that, young people have the natural inclination that Freire was referring to: act upon, and learn about how to change the world—one's own world and beyond. In so doing they will discover why we are on this planet, in this universe. Act upon, learn about, shape and be shaped by the world. Education never had a better role. In a real sense everything is alive. The physical and social worlds are our partners. The cosmos is great when we help make it so. After all, education is only wonderful when you are a proactive participant in figuring out why you and others are in this universe. You can be big and small at the same time. At least that's my life!

Coda

I dedicated this book to Vince, Mary, Gerry, and Harry—seen and unseen deeply positive forces in my life. But they never were really there the way that I envisaged them were they? They were surreal too.

Was this book easy to write? The answer is yes, but not in the way I expected. It was an emotional and intellectual cleansing—a detoxification of the mind and the soul. It gives me solitude. It makes me feel simultaneously alone, and part of the universe. It gives me meaning at a level so profound that it is surreal. It never happened, but it did!

As I end this book I am sipping my favorite Irish Whiskey—Writers' Tears. Writers' tears are often ones that comingle sadness and joy in a way that both are pleasurable. A life immersed in change can do that to you. When you spend a lot of time in high profile situations being seen as a leader, you come to think that you are greater than you actually are. I do not think I am great. I never wanted to be better than Bucky Bully—a freewheeling 5-year-old. Say it fast and maybe it can happen to you.

Books by Michael Fullan

The meaning of educational change 1982
What's worth fighting for in the principalship (2nd Ed.) 1988
The new meaning of educational change (2nd Ed.) 1991
Successful school improvement 1992
What's worth fighting for? Working together for your school 1992
Change forces 1993
What's worth fighting for out there? 1998
The rise and stall of teacher education reform (G. Galluzzo, P. Morris, & N. Watson)
    1998
Change forces: The sequel 1999
Leading in a culture of change 2001a
The new meaning of educational change (3rd Ed.) 2001b
Change forces with a vengeance 2003a
The moral imperative of school leadership 2003b
Leading in a culture of change: Personal action guide and workbook 2004
Leadership and sustainability: System thinkers in action 2005
Learning places (with C. St Germain) 2006
Turnaround leadership 2006
Breakthrough (with P. Hill and C. Crévola) 2006
The new meaning of educational change (4th Ed.) 2007
The six secrets of change 2008
Change wars (Edited with A. Hargreaves) 2009
Turnaround leadership for higher education (with G. Scott) 2009
Realization (with L. Sharratt) 2009
The challenge of change (Edited) 2009

All systems go 2010a
Motion leadership: The skinny on becoming change savvy 2010b
Change leader 2011a
The moral imperative realized 2011c
Professional capital: Transforming teaching in every school (with A. Hargreaves)
    2012
Putting FACES on the data: What great leaders do! (with L. Sharratt) 2012
Motion leadership in action 2013b
Stratosphere: Integrating technology, pedagogy, and change knowledge 2013c
Cultures built to last: Systemic PLCs at work (with R. Dufour) 2013
The principal: Three keys to maximizing impact 2014c
Big-city school reforms (with A. Boyle) 2014
Freedom to change 2015
Evaluating and assessing tools in the digital swamp (with K. Donnelly) 2015
The new meaning of educational change (5th Ed.) 2016
Coherence (with J. Quinn) 2016
Taking action guide to building coherence (with J. Quinn and E. Adam) 2016
Leadership: Key competencies for whole system change (with L. Kirtman) 2016
Indelible leadership: Always leave them learning 2016a
The power of unstoppable momentum: Key drivers to revolutionize your district
    (with M. Edwards) 2017
Deep learning: Engage the world change the world (with J. Quinn & J. McEachen)
    2018
Surreal change 2018

Bibliography

Ahtiainen, R. (2017). Shades of change in Fullan's and Hargreaves's models. University of Helsinki: Doctoral dissertation.

Atlantic Rim Collaboratory. (2017). *ARC declarations*. Retrieved from http://atrico.org/data/uploads/2017/01/arc-declaration.pdf

Charters, W. & Jones, J. (1973). On the neglect of the independent variable. Unpublished paper: University of Oregon.

Chu, L. (2017). *Little soldiers: An American boy, a Chinese school, and the global race to achieve*. New York, NY: Harper Collins.

Dalin, P. (1978). *Limits to educational change*. London, UK: Macmillan Press.

Dufour, R. & Fullan, M. (2013). *Cultures Built to last: Systemic PLCs at work*. Bloomington, IN: Solution Tree.

Earl, L., Watson, N., Levin, B., Leithwood, K., & Fullan, M. (2003). *Watching and learning 3; final report of the external evaluation of England's national literacy and numeracy strategies*. Toronto, Canada: OISE/UT.

Elmore, R. (1995). Getting to scale with good education practice. *Harvard Education Review 66(1)*, 1–26.

Elmore, R. & Burney, D. (1999). Investing in teacher learning. In L. Darling-Hammond & G. Sykes (Eds.), *Teaching as the learning profession*. pp. 236–291. San Francisco, CA: Jossey-Bass.

Freire, P. (2000). *Pedagogy of the oppressed*. New York, NY: Bloomsbury.

Fromm, E. (1969). *Escape from freedom*. Second Edition. New York, NY: Holt Paperbacks.

Fullan, M. (1966). Unit autonomy in India. University of Toronto: Master of Arts Thesis.

Fullan, M. (1969). Workers' receptivity to industrial change in different technological settings. University of Toronto: Doctoral dissertation.

Fullan, M. (1972). Overview of the innovative processes and the user. *Interchange* 3(*3*), 1–46.

Fullan, M. (1982). *The meaning of educational change.* New York, NY: Teachers College Press.

Fullan, M. (1988). *What's worth fighting for in the principalship?* Toronto, Canada: Ontario Public School Teachers' Federation.

Fullan, M. (with Steigelbauer). (1991). *The new meaning of educational change.* Second Edition. New York, NY: Teachers College Press.

Fullan, M. (1993). *Change forces.* London, UK: Falmer Press.

Fullan, M. (1997). *What's worth fighting for in the principalship?* New York, NY: Teachers College Press.

Fullan, M. (1999). *Change forces: The sequel.* London, UK: RoutledgeFalmer.

Fullan, M. (2000). The return of large-scale reform. *Journal of Educational Change* 1(*1*), 5–27.

Fullan, M. (2001a). *Leading in a culture of change.* San Francisco, CA: Jossey-Bass.

Fullan, M. (2001b). *The new meaning of educational change.* Third Edition. New York, NY: Teachers College Press.

Fullan, M. (2003a). *Change forces with a vengeance.* London, UK: Routledge-Falmer.

Fullan, M. (2003b). *The moral imperative of school leadership.* Thousand Oaks, CA: Corwin Press; Toronto, Canada: Ontario Principals' Council.

Fullan, M. (2005). *Leadership and sustainability: System thinkers in action.* Thousand Oaks, CA: Corwin Press; Toronto, Canada: Ontario Principals' Council.

Fullan, M. (2006). *Turnaround leadership.* San Francisco, CA: Jossey-Bass.

Fullan, M. (2007). *The new meaning of educational change.* Second Edition. New York, NY: Teachers College Press.

Fullan, M. (2008). *The six secrets of change.* San Francisco, CA: Jossey-Bass.

Fullan, M. (2010a). *All systems go: The change imperative for whole school reform.* Thousand Oaks, CA: Corwin.

Fullan, M. (2010b). *Motion leadership: The skinny on becoming change savvy.* Thousand Oaks, CA: Corwin Press.

Fullan, M. (2011a). *Change leader: Learning to do what matters most.* San Francisco, CA: Jossey-Bass.

Fullan, M. (2011b). *Choosing the wrong drivers for whole system reform. Seminar Series 204.* Melbourne, Australia: Center for Strategic Education.

Fullan, M. (2011c). *The moral imperative realized.* Thousand Oaks, CA: Corwin.

Fullan, M. (2013a). *Great to excellent: Launching the next stage of Ontario's education agenda.* Retrieved from www.edu.gov.on.ca/eng/document/reports/FullanReport_EN_07.pdf

Fullan, M. (2013b). *Motion leadership in action.* Thousand Oaks, CA: Corwin.

Fullan, M. (2013c). *Stratosphere: Integrating technology, pedagogy, and change knowledge.* Toronto, Canada: Pearson.

Fullan, M. (2014a). *California's golden opportunity: A status note.* Retrieved from www.michaelfullan.ca

Fullan, M. (2014b). *Motion leadership film series*. Retrieved from www. michaelfullan.ca

Fullan, M. (2014c). *The principal: Three keys to maximizing impact*. San Francisco, CA: Jossey-Bass.

Fullan, M. (2015). *Freedom to change: Four strategies to put your inner drive into overdrive*. San Francisco, CA: Jossey-Bass.

Fullan, M. (2016a). *Indelible leadership: Always leave them learning*. Thousand Oaks, CA: Corwin Press.

Fullan, M. (2016b). *The new meaning of educational change*. Fifth Edition. New York, NY: Teachers College Press.

Fullan, M. & Boyle, A. (2014). *Big-city school reforms: Lessons from New York, Toronto, and London*. New York, NY: Teachers College Press.

Fullan, M. & Connelly, F. (1987). *Teacher education in Ontario*. Toronto, Canada: Ministry of Education.

Fullan, M. & Donnelly, K. (2015). *Alive in the swamp: Assessing digital innovation in education*. London, UK: NESTA; New York, NY: New Schools Venture Fund.

Fullan, M. & Edwards, M.A. (2017). *The power of unstoppable momentum: Key drivers to revolutionize your district*. Bloomington, IN: Solution Tree.

Fullan, M. & Hargreaves, A. (1996). *What's worth fighting for in your school?* New York, NY: Teachers' College Press.

Fullan, M. & Hargreaves, A. (2016). *Bringing the profession back in*. Oxford, OH: Learning Forward.

Fullan, M., Hill, P., & Crévola, C. (2006). *Breakthrough*. Thousand Oaks, CA: Corwin.

Fullan, M. & Langworthy, M. (2014). *A rich seam: How new pedagogies find deep learning*. London, UK: Pearson.

Fullan, M. & Loubser, J.J. (1972). Education and adaptive capacity. *American Sociological Association* 45(*3*), 271–287.

Fullan, M. & Pomfret, A. (1977). Research on curriculum and instruction implementation. *Review of Educational Research* 47(*1*), 335–397.

Fullan, M. & Quinn, J. (2016). *Coherence: The right drivers in action for schools, districts, and systems*. Thousand Oaks, CA: Corwin Press.

Fullan, M., Quinn, J., & McEachen, J. (2018). *Deep learning: Engage the world change the world*. Thousand Oaks, CA: Corwin Press.

Fullan, M. & Rincón-Gallardo, S. (2016). Developing high quality public education in Canada: The case of Ontario. In F. Adamson, B. Astrand, & L. Darling-Hammond (Eds.), *Global education reform: How privatization and public investment influence education outcomes*. pp. 169–193. New York, NY: Routledge.

Fullan, M., Rincón-Gallardo, S., & Hargreaves, A. (2015). Professional capital as accountability. *Education Policy Analysis Archives* 23(*15*), 1–18.

Fullan, M. & Scott, G. (2009). *Turnaround leadership for higher education*. San Francisco, CA: Jossey-Bass.

Goodlad, J., Klein, M., & Associates. (1970). *Behind the classroom door.* Worthington, OH: Charles A. Jones.

Gross, N., Giacquinta, J., & Bernstein, M. (1971). *Implementing organizational innovations: A sociological analysis of planned educational change.* New York, NY: Basic Books.

Hargreaves, A. & Braun, H. (2012). *Leading for all: A research report of the development, design, implementation and impact of Ontario's "Essential for Some, Good for All" initiative.* Boston, MA: Boston College.

Hargreaves, A. & Fullan, M. (1996). *What's worth fighting for in your school?* New York, NY: Teachers College Press.

Hargreaves, A. & Fullan, M. (1998). *What's worth fighting for out there?* New York, NY: Teachers College Press.

Hargreaves, A. & Fullan, M. (2012). *Professional capital: Transforming teaching in every school.* New York, NY: Teachers College Press.

Kirtman, L. & Fullan, M. (2015). *Leadership: Key competencies for whole system change.* Bloomington, IN: Solution Tree.

Leithwood, K., Fullan, M., & Watson, N. (2003). *The schools we need: A new blueprint for Ontario. Final Report.* Retrieved September 27, 2017 from https://tspace.library.utoronto.ca/retrieve/871/SWN.pdf

Maximum City. (2017). Retrieved from http://maximumcity.ca. Toronto, Canada: Author.

Ng, P.T. (2017). *Learning from Singapore: The power of paradoxes.* London, UK: Routledge.

Ontario Ministry of Education (2014). *Achieving excellence: A renewed vision for education in Ontario.* Author.

Ontario Ministry of Education (2017). Ontario's Education Equity Action Plan. Author.

Pascal, C. (2009). *With our best future in mind: Implementing early learning in Ontario.* Commissioner's Report to the Premier of Ontario.

Pelletier, J. (2017). *Ontario's full day kindergarten: A bold public policy initiative.* Retrieved from https://drive.google.com/file/d/0B88CdMnXfcrENj-hyRXAtMW00OGM/view

Robinson, V. (2011). *Student-centered leadership.* San Francisco, CA: Jossey-Bass.

Robinson, V. (2018). *Reduce change to increase improvement.* Thousand Oaks, CA: Corwin Press.

Sahlberg, P. (2018). *FinnishED leadership.* Thousand Oaks, CA: Corwin Press.

Sarason, S.B. (1971). *The culture of the school and the problem of change.* Boston, MA: Allyn & Bacon.

Sarason, S.B. (1982). *Culture of the school and the problem of change.* Second Edition. Boston, MA: Allyn & Bacon.

Schleicher, A. (in press). *World class.* Paris: Organization for Economic Co-operation and Development.

Sharratt, L. & Fullan, M. (2009). *Realization.* Thousand Oaks, CA: Corwin.

Sharratt, L. & Fullan, M. (2012). *Putting FACES on the data: What great leaders do!* Thousand Oaks, CA: Corwin.

Shirley, D. (2017). *The new imperatives of education change.* New York, NY: Routledge.

Truth and Reconciliation Canada. (2015). *Honouring the truth, reconciling for the future: Summary of the final report of the Truth and Reconciliation Commission of Canada.* Winnipeg, Canada: Truth and Reconciliation Commission of Canada.

United States. National Commission on Excellence in Education. Department of Education. (1983). *A nation at risk: The imperative for educational reform.* Report to the Nation and the Secretary of Education. Washington.

Index